Horrors of Judgement Day

A concise and comprehensive commentary of Sūrah Naba, Sūrah Nāzi'āt and Sūrah Abas which discusses the catastrophes and horrors of the Hereafter.

By
Shaykh Mufti Saiful Islām

© Copyright by JKN Publications

Published in November 2015
ISBN 978-1-909114-16-6

British Library Cataloguing in Publication Data
A catalogue record for this book is available from the British Library.

Publisher's Note:

Every care and attention has been put into the production of this book. If however, you find any errors, they are our own, for which we seek Allāh's ﷻ forgiveness and the reader's pardon.

Published by:

JKN Publications
118 Manningham Lane
Bradford
West Yorkshire
BD8 7JF
United Kingdom

t: +44 (0) 1274 308 456 | w: www.jkn.org.uk | e: info@jkn.org.uk

Book Title: Horrors of Judgement Day

Author: Shaykh Mufti Saiful Islām

Printed by Mega Printing in Turkey

"In the Name of Allāh, the Most Beneficent,
the Most Merciful"

Contents

Contents

Introduction

All praises are due to Allāh 🕮. May peace, salutations and blessings be upon our guide and mentor, the final and beloved Prophet Muhammad 🕮, upon his noble Sahābah 🕮, Tābi'een and those who follow their noble lifestyles until the Day of Judgement. Āmeen!

The Holy Qur'ān states regarding the Holy Prophet 🕮,
"We have not sent you (O' Muhammad) but as a carrier of good tidings and as a warner to all mankind." (34:28)

Mufti Taqi Uthmāni states that this verse implies to all humans, wherever and in whatever age they are living. The Prophethood encompasses all periods and ages till the Day of Judgement. The Holy Prophet's 🕮 teachings and injunctions shall remain valid, effective and in force till the Day of Judgement. These teachings of the Holy Prophet 🕮 consist of two aspects:

- Prescribing the rules of the Shari'ah concerning lawful, unlawful, desirable, permissible and other aspects.
- Predicting the events which will confront the Ummah in the times to come and how the Ummah should tackle these events, in this world and the Hereafter.

The Horrors of the Day of Judgement have already been pictured to us by our beloved Prophet 🕮 through the Holy Qur'ān and Ahādeeth. On the Day of Judgement, every individual, male or female, will be resurrected to account for their lives. Allāh 🕮 describes this event in the Holy Qur'ān,

"On that Day people will come forward in separate groups to be shown their deeds. Whoever has done an atom weight of good will

see it and whoever has done an atom's weight of evil will see it."
(99:6-8)

Allāh ﷻ will weigh everyone's good and bad actions according to His Mercy and His Justice, forgiving many sins and multiplying the reward for many noble deeds. One who excels in goodness, will be rewarded generously but one whose evils and wrongs outweigh his virtues, will be punished.

In this book, my beloved Shaykh, Mufti Saiful Islām, explains the horrors of the Day of Judgement beautifully, through the commentary of Sūrah Naba, Sūrah Nā'ziyāt and Sūrah Abas, as the theme of these three Sūrahs are related and they were all revealed at a similar Makkan period. These Sūrahs emphasise the certainty of the Day of Judgement and lay stress on its occurrence by emphatic statements which relate to the resurrection. They point to some of the frightening and dreadful incidents of that Day. They mention various countless powers of Allāh ﷻ, which exist in the heavens and on the earth. They describe many other aspects of the horrible events to occur on that Great Day and the painful end of the wrong-doers in contrast to the rewards of the righteous servants of Allāh ﷻ.

May Allāh ﷻ accept the efforts of all those who have participated in the writing and compilation of this book, especially my beloved teacher and Shaykh, Mufti Saiful Islām and reward them in the life of this world and the Hereafter. Āmeen!

Maulānā Ismāeel Aziz
Graduate of JKN
November 2015/Muharram 1437

Sūrah Naba

The News

Revealed in Makkah

بِسْمِ اللهِ الرَّحْمٰنِ الرَّحِيْمِ

In the Name of Allāh , the Most Compassionate, the Most Merciful.

عَمَّ يَتَسَآءَلُوۡنَ . عَنِ النَّبَإِ الْعَظِيۡمِ . الَّذِيۡ هُمۡ فِيۡهِ مُخۡتَلِفُوۡنَ . كَلَّا سَيَعۡلَمُوۡنَ . ثُمَّ كَلَّا سَيَعۡلَمُوۡنَ .

1. What do they ask about?
2. About the great news.
3. Concerning which they differ?
4. Take heed! They will soon come to know.
5. Take heed again! They will soon come to know.

Imām Qurtubi ◈ narrates that some members of the Quraysh tribe were once having a discussion. When it was mentioned that the Holy Qur'ān spoke about the Day of Judgement, some of them accepted while others did not. It was with reference to this discussion that Allāh ◈ revealed the verse.

عَمَّ يَتَسَآءَلُوۡنَ

"What do they ask about?"

Allāh ◈ Himself, replies to the question when He says,

عَنِ النَّبَإِ الْعَظِيۡمِ . الَّذِيۡ هُمۡ فِيۡهِ مُخۡتَلِفُوۡنَ

"About the great news (Day of Judgement) concerning which they differ."

8

While some of them believed in the Day of Judgement, others did not. Allāh ﷻ says,

$$كَلَّا سَيَعْلَمُوْنَ . ثُمَّ كَلَّا سَيَعْلَمُوْنَ$$

"Take heed! They will soon come to know."

Allāh ﷻ then repeats, **"Take heed again! They will soon come to know."**

They will realise the error of their ways when the Day of Reckoning does take place, but then it will be too late.

Hifz Class
Sūrah Naba (The News) was revealed in Makkah which consists of 40 verses. I can remember that it was the first Sūrah that I memorised in my Hifz class back in 1985 in Tawak'kulia Jāmi Masjid, Bradford. To encourage the students of the Hifz Class, our head Imām and principal of the Institute, Maulāna Ashraf Ali Sikder Sāhib, who is present within our midst (May Allāh ﷻ prolong his life, give us the opportunity to benefit from his knowledge and keep him healthy for many years to come) used to put his signature in the attendance register next to our names after every ten verses. We would look forward to that well furnished and beautiful signature after reciting every ten verses to our Hifz class teacher, Hāfiz Jalāl-Uddin Sāhib (may Allāh ﷻ bless him with a healthy life).

Regret of the Disbelievers
In this Sūrah, Allāh ﷻ mentions initially, about the differences people hold regarding the Day of Judgement. Then, He makes it clear that we should take heed that the Day of Judgement will surely take place and then, all the contradictions and differences will be settled, but then it will be too late.

In Sūrah Al-Mu'minoon verse 99, Allāh ﷻ says in reference to the disbe-

9

lievers,

حَتَّىٰٓ إِذَا جَآءَ أَحَدَهُمُ الْمَوْتُ قَالَ رَبِّ ارْجِعُونِ

"(The disbelievers continue the perpetration of disbelief and behaving stubbornly) until the time arrives when death comes to anyone of them, then (when he sees the punishment in store for him) he says 'O' my Lord! Allow me to return (to the world).'"(23:99)

Why?

لَعَلِّيٓ أَعْمَلُ صَالِحًا فِيمَا تَرَكْتُ

"So that I may perform good deeds in that (worldly life) which I have left behind." (23:100)

What does Allāh ﷻ say?

كَلَّآ إِنَّهَا كَلِمَةٌ هُوَ قَآئِلُهَا

"Never (they will never do as they say)! It (their promise to lead better lives) is merely a statement that they speak (an empty prom- ise)." (23:100)

What is going to happen now? Allāh ﷻ concludes,

وَمِن وَرَآئِهِم بَرْزَخٌ إِلَىٰ يَوْمِ يُبْعَثُونَ

(They will be unable to return to the world because) behind them is 'Barzakh' (a barrier preventing their return which will remain in place, referring to the life of the grave) until the Day that they are resurrected (on the Day of Judgement) (23:100)

As Muslims, we need to prepare ourselves before the great news (Day of Reckoning).

Naba is from the root letters Noon, Bā and Alif from which the word Nabi (i.e. Prophet) is derived, the plural of which is Anbiyā. These are the special people who have been chosen to convey the great news and relay the information from Allāh ﷻ to the people.

Alhamdulillāh, through our beloved Prophet Muhammad ﷺ, we have received all the news of the Hereafter so that we could make our preparations.

$$ أَلَمۡ نَجۡعَلِ الۡأَرۡضَ مِهَادًا . وَّالۡجِبَالَ أَوۡتَادًا . وَّخَلَقۡنَاكُمۡ أَزۡوَاجًا $$

6. Have We not made the earth a bedding?
7. The mountains pegs?
8. And created you in pairs?

Ponder Over the Creation

Allāh ﷻ mentions some of His creations which are there for all to see. By pondering over these, man will realise Allāh's ﷻ great power and will understand that the Being who created such phenomenal things must certainly have the power to resurrect people on the Day of Judgement. Allāh ﷻ asks, **"Have We not made the earth a bedding, the mountains pegs?** Because the mountains prevent the earth from shaking, man is able to stand, walk and travel easily on earth.

Allāh ﷻ encourages us to look around to see His great creative powers.

He says,

$$ أَفَلَا يَنۡظُرُوۡنَ إِلَى الۡإِبِلِ كَيۡفَ خُلِقَتۡ $$

"Have they (mankind) not looked at the camel and seen how it was created (perfectly, adapted to the harsh climate of the desert with so many features, qualities and capabilities)?" (88:17)

11

وَاِلَى السَّمَآءِ كَيْفَ رُفِعَتْ

"And (have they not looked) at the sky, how it was raised (so high without any supports)?" (88:18)

وَاِلَى الْجِبَالِ كَيْفَ نُصِبَتْ

"And (have they not looked) at the mountains, how they were placed firmly into the earth with their bulk underground)?" (88:19)

وَاِلَى الْأَرْضِ كَيْفَ سُطِحَتْ

"And (have they not looked) at the earth, how it was spread out (with large tracks of land that seem flat despite the spherical shape of the earth)?" (88:20)

Allāh ﷻ has also created spouses for men so that men may marry, have loving companions through the difficulties of life and have contentment. How beautifully He mentions this blessing and favour in Sūrah Room, verse 21:

وَمِنْ آيَاتِهِ أَنْ خَلَقَ لَكُمْ مِنْ أَنْفُسِكُمْ أَزْوَاجًا لِتَسْكُنُوا إِلَيْهَا وَجَعَلَ بَيْنَكُمْ مَّوَدَّةً وَّرَحْمَةً

"Also among His Signs is that He created spouses for you from your-selves (from your own species) so that you may find solace (peace and rest) with her and has placed (blessed you with tremendous) love (most clearly seen during youth and adulthood) and (blessed you with a great deal of) mercy (most clearly appreciated during old age) be-tween you." (30:21)

Allāh ﷻ concludes the verse by reminding us,

$$إِنَّ فِيْ ذٰلِكَ لَاٰيَاتٍ لِّقَوْمٍ يَّتَفَكَّرُوْنَ$$

"There are certainly Signs in this for people who contemplate (people who have insight)"

$$وَّجَعَلْنَا نَوْمَكُمْ سُبَاتًا . وَّجَعَلْنَا الَّيْلَ لِبَاسًا . وَّجَعَلْنَا النَّهَارَ مَعَاشًا . وَّبَنَيْنَا فَوْقَكُمْ سَبْعًا شِدَادًا$$

9. And We have made sleep a means of rest.
10. The night a drape.
11. And the day a means of earning livelihood.

Sleep - A Great Blessing

In verse 9, Allāh ﷻ says,

$$وَّجَعَلْنَا نَوْمَكُمْ سُبَاتًا$$

"And We have made sleep a means of rest."

Man gets physically and mentally tired during his daily activities and needs sleep to recuperate his energy. After a good night's rest, man again has the energy to continue his daily activities. The Arabic word 'Subāta' translated as a means of rest, literally refers to cutting something. This word aptly describes sleep because the voluntary movements of a person's limbs terminate while he sleeps and his fatigue is alleviated.

In verses 10 and 11, He says that He made, **"The night a drape and the day a means of earning livelihood?"** Man has the night to rest at home and the light of the day in which to earn a living. Therefore, the night and the day are great bounties of Allāh ﷻ. One can well imagine the

13

difficulty if night had to be perpetual or if day had to be perpetual.

Allāh ﷻ mentions this great favour in Sūrah Al-Qasas,

قُلْ أَرَءَيْتُمْ إِنْ جَعَلَ اللهُ عَلَيْكُمُ الَّيْلَ سَرْمَدًا إِلَى يَوْمِ الْقِيَامَةِ مَنْ إِلَهٌ غَيْرُ اللهِ يَأْتِيْكُمْ بِضِيَآءٍ أَفَلَا تَسْمَعُوْنَ

"Tell me, if Allāh makes the night perpetual (unending) for you until the Day of Judgement, which god besides Him can bring light to you? Can you not hear (listen to this with the intention of understanding and accepting)?"

For this reason, it is always beneficial, Islamically as well as medically, to take rest at night and carry out our activities in the day time. Those who try to reverse this divine system will not be successful in their aims and objectives. A few hours of sleep at night is much more beneficial than long hours of sleep in the day time. Our beloved Prophet ﷺ has prayed for Barakah (blessings) for the Ummah in the early morning. Hence, we should have value for the early morning time. Other nations have taken this on board and have progressed immensely in their worldly pursuits. All our answers and solutions to our worldly and Deeny problems have been mentioned in the Holy Qur'ān and Ahādeeth. If only we take heed!

وَبَنَيْنَا فَوْقَكُمْ سَبْعًا شِدَادًا . وَّجَعَلْنَا سِرَاجًا وَّهَّاجًا . وَأَنْزَلْنَا مِنَ الْمُعْصِرَاتِ مَاءً ثَجَّاجًا . لِنُخْرِجَ بِهِ حَبًّا وَّنَبَاتًا . وَّجَنَّاتٍ أَلْفَافًا

12. (And have We not) made seven powerful skies above you.
13. And We made a bright lantern.
14. And We sent torrential rains from the laden clouds.
15. To extract with it seeds and plants.
16. And dense gardens.

Great Creations

Allāh ﷻ says, "(And have We not) made seven powerful skies above you and made a bright lantern i.e. the sun." Generating its own light, the sun provides the earth with innumerable benefits apart from light. It provides heat and allows plants and vegetation to grow.

In Sūrah Mulk it states,

الَّذِيْ خَلَقَ سَبْعَ سَمَاوَاتٍ طِبَاقًا مَا تَرٰى فِيْ خَلْقِ الرَّحْمٰنِ مِنْ تَفَاوُتٍ فَارْجِعِ الْبَصَرَ
هَلْ تَرٰى مِنْ فُطُوْرٍ

"He has created the seven heavens in layers. You will not see any inconsistency (defects) in Allāh's creation. Look again. Do you see any cracks (in the sky)?" (67:03)

These skies are so powerful that till today, there has been no need to carry out repairs or any servicing.

In Sūrah Ra'ad it states,

اللّٰهُ الَّذِيْ رَفَعَ السَّمَاوَاتِ بِغَيْرِ عَمَدٍ تَرَوْنَهَا ثُمَّ اسْتَوٰى عَلَى الْعَرْشِ وَسَخَّرَ الشَّمْسَ
وَالْقَمَرَ كُلٌّ يَّجْرِيْ لِأَجَلٍ مُّسَمًّى

"It is Allāh Who raised the skies without any pillars that you see (no pillars are visible because there are none), then turned his attention to the Throne and subjected (controlled) the sun and the moon. Each (the sun and the moon) runs to its appointed term. (They follow their courses in space and will do as Allāh wills)." (13:02)

All these creations point to a Mighty Creator which is Allāh ﷻ. He has assigned everything precisely in their places.

15

In Sūrah Yāseen, Allāh ﷻ says,

وَالشَّمْسُ تَجْرِي لِمُسْتَقَرٍّ لَّهَا ذَٰلِكَ تَقْدِيرُ الْعَزِيزِ الْعَلِيمِ

"The sun travels towards its destination (within its orbit without straying from course). This is the (perfect) arrangement of the Mighty, the All-Knowing." (36:38)

Allāh ﷻ uses the rain as a means of growing plants, many of which form man's staple diet. Among the many things that rain also grows is fodder for animals which in turn provide man with food, milk, hide, transport and labour. The Arabic word "Al-Fāfa" (translated above as dense) refers to trees, the branches of which twine into each other as they grow.

Just ponder over the magnificent system and cycle of Allāh ﷻ in regards to the rain.

أَلَمْ تَرَ أَنَّ اللَّهَ يُزْجِي سَحَابًا ثُمَّ يُؤَلِّفُ بَيْنَهُ ثُمَّ يَجْعَلُهُ رُكَامًا فَتَرَى الْوَدْقَ يَخْرُجُ مِنْ خِلَالِهِ وَيُنَزِّلُ مِنَ السَّمَاءِ مِنْ جِبَالٍ فِيهَا مِنْ بَرَدٍ فَيُصِيبُ بِهِ مَنْ يَشَاءُ وَيَصْرِفُهُ عَنْ مَّنْ يَشَاءُ يَكَادُ سَنَا بَرْقِهِ يَذْهَبُ بِالْأَبْصَارِ

"Do you not see that Allāh gently drives the clouds towards the place where He intends the rain to fall, then condenses (gathers) them (causes the water to vapour to form into water droplets) and stacks them with layers, after which (when Allāh decides), you will see rain falling from between them? Then, from the mountainous clouds in the sky, Allāh showers down (abundantly) some ice (hail, snow), by which He strikes whoever (and whatever) He wills (thereby causing harm to whoever He wills) and averts from whoever (or whatever) He wills. The flash of His lightning (is so bright that it) can almost snatch away eyesight (however Allāh protects the peoples eyesight)." (24:43)

16

Regarding the plants and seeds, Allāh ﷻ mentions the phenomenal structure of them in Sūrah Ra'ad,

وَفِي الْأَرْضِ قِطَعٌ مُّتَجَاوِرَاتٌ وَّجَنَّاتٌ مِّنْ أَعْنَابٍ وَّزَرْعٌ وَّنَخِيلٌ صِنْوَانٌ وَّغَيْرُ صِنْوَانٍ يُّسْقَىٰ بِمَاءٍ وَّاحِدٍ وَّنُفَضِّلُ بَعْضَهَا عَلَىٰ بَعْضٍ فِي الْأُكُلِ

"On the earth there are neighbouring tracts of land (that have opposing characteristics despite being next to each other), orchards of grapes, plantations and date palms, some of which grow in clusters while others do not (they stand alone). All (the grapes, plantations and date palms) are irrigated by one (the same) water (yet the results are so diverse). (In addition to the various types and appearances of these plants) We accord distinction (excellence) to one over the other in eating (in texture, taste and nutritional value)." (13:4)

إِنَّ يَوْمَ الْفَصْلِ كَانَ مِيقَاتًا . يَّوْمَ يُنْفَخُ فِي الصُّورِ فَتَأْتُونَ أَفْوَاجًا

17. Verily the Day of Judgement has been fixed
18. The Day when the trumpet will be blown and you will come in large groups.

Day of Judgement

If we ponder over the great creation of Allāh ﷻ and His recount of some manifestations of this immense power in the opening verses of Sūrah Naba, then we will realise that Allāh ﷻ is certainly capable of resurrecting the dead on the Day of Judgement. Allāh ﷻ makes it clear that the Day of Judgement will neither be preponed or postponed even though there may be people who deny its advent.

Allāh ﷻ says,
"Verily the Day of Judgement has been fixed, the Day when the trum-

pet will be blown and you will come large groups. (Every generation from the time of Sayyidunā Ādam will present themselves for the reckoning and they will arrive from their graves in large numbers)."

In Sūrah Dukhān, Allāh ﷻ reiterates the same message,

$$\text{إِنَّ يَوْمَ الْفَصْلِ مِيقَاتُهُمْ أَجْمَعِينَ . يَوْمَ لَا يُغْنِي مَوْلًى عَنْ مَّوْلًى شَيْئًا وَّلَا هُمْ يُنْصَرُونَ . إِلَّا مَنْ رَّحِمَ اللّٰهُ إِنَّهُ هُوَ الْعَزِيزُ الرَّحِيمُ}$$

"Indeed, the Day of Judgement has been stipulated for all of them. (It is) the Day when one companion will be of no benefit to another, neither shall they be assisted except those whom Allāh has mercy on. Indeed, He is the Almighty, Most Merciful." (44:40:42)

Describing the horrific scenario of Judgement Day in Sūrah Yāseen, Allāh ﷻ pronounces,

$$\text{وَنُفِخَ فِي الصُّورِ فَإِذَا هُم مِّنَ الْأَجْدَاثِ إِلَىٰ رَبِّهِمْ يَنسِلُونَ . قَالُوا يَا وَيْلَنَا مَن بَعَثَنَا مِن مَّرْقَدِنَا هَٰذَا مَا وَعَدَ الرَّحْمَٰنُ وَصَدَقَ الْمُرْسَلُونَ . إِن كَانَتْ إِلَّا صَيْحَةً وَّاحِدَةً فَإِذَا هُمْ جَمِيعٌ لَّدَيْنَا مُحْضَرُونَ}$$

"The trumpet will be blown (to signal the arrival of Qiyāmah) and they will rush to their Lord (for reckoning) from their graves." (Overcome with grief and worry) they will say, "Alas, who has raised us from our graves? This is what Rahmān promised and the Messengers spoke the truth." It (the arrival of Qiyāmah) will be (signalled by) one single scream, after which they will appear before Us (to account for their actions in the world)."

18

Allāh ﷻ explains to us in many different verses about the catastrophes and terror which will grip every person. The Holy Qur'ān relates that we will be coming in different groups with our Prophets and leaders.

In Sūrah Bani-Isrā'eel, verse 71, Allāh ﷻ eloquently says,

يَوۡمَ نَدۡعُوۡا كُلَّ أُنَاسٍۭ بِإِمَامِهِمۡ

"(Do not forget) the Day when We will call every person by his Imām (by his Prophet and his record of deeds)."

Shāh Abdul Aziz Muhaddith Dehlawi ؒ mentions in his Tafseer Kitāb, 'Tafseer Azeezi,' under the commentary of this verse: Every group, according to their beliefs, will be in separate rows - Jews, Christians, Hindus, Zoroastrians will be in separate rows. Then, in the Muslims there will be different rows and groups. Those who are righteous will be separate from sinners. Those who are punctual in their Salāh will be in one row; the ones who observed the fast will be in one row. Then, according to the Akhlāq (character), people will be in different rows and groups. Those who are arrogant will be separate, those who are humble will be separate, those who persevered will be separate and those who expressed gratitude will be separate. Each group leader will take his people and advance towards the Plain of Resurrection. In the Ahādeeth, it mentions different signs of these different groups e.g. those who cheated and deceived will have flags raised from their buttocks. Those who stole from the spoils of war will have the item stuck around their necks. Those who were martyred in the path of Allāh ﷻ will have fresh blood on their wounds and musk fragrance emitting from them. According to different narrations, many people will be transformed into the appearances of animals.

Different Groups

Imām Sa'labi 🙾 mentions in his Tafseer that one day the Companions asked the Holy Prophet 🙾 regarding these large groups mentioned in this Sūrah. The Holy Prophet 🙾 said that ten groups will be coming from this Ummah:

1) The 1st group will be in the appearance of monkeys - these were the tale bearers.

2) The 2nd group will be in the appearance of pigs - these were the ones who took bribes.

3) The 3rd group will be raised upside down, head on the floor and feet raised towards the heavens with the angels dragging them by their faces. These are the people who consumed usury.

4) The 4th group of people will be raised blind - these are the scholars and judges who issued wrong verdicts and committed injustice in their judgements.

5) The 5th group will be raised dumb - these are the people who expressed arrogance and pride in their worship.

6) The 6th group will be raised whilst their tongues will be over their mouths and dangling from their chests. A foul smell will emit from them that will cause disturbance and inconvenience to all the people on the Plain of Resurrection. These will be scholars whose deeds were in conflict to their speeches.

7) The 7th group will be raised without heads and legs - these are the people who used to inflict pain upon animals unjustly and used to trou-

ble their neighbours.

8) The 8th group will be raised hanging upon crosses of fire - these are the people who passed the secret matters of people to the tyrant rulers to impose hardships upon them.

9) The 9th group will be raised in a state that a very severe stench will be emitting from their bodies which will disturb all the people on the Plain of Resurrection. These will be the people who fulfilled their desires in the worldly pursuits and spent their wealth extravagantly in the wrong avenues.

10) The 10th group will be raised whilst wearing clothes made of tar clinged to their bodies - these will be the people who were arrogant and boastful.

Contrary to this, those who are pious will have faces shining like the moon on the forteenth night. Some will be like the glittering stars, some will be seated on Mimbar (pulpits) made of celestial light and others will be seated on mountains of musk and saffron.

May Allāh 泌 make us from the righteous and save us from all types of evil. Āmeen!

Gigantic Mountains

وَفُتِحَتِ السَّمَاءُ فَكَانَتْ أَبْوَابًا . وَّسُيِّرَتِ الْجِبَالُ فَكَانَتْ سَرَابًا

19) The sky will be opened and will become many doors.
20) The mountains will be made to fly and will be reduced to dust.

Allāh ﷻ further describes the scene of the Day when He says,

"The sky will be opened and will be many doors (letting the way for the angels to come down with all the record books). The mountains will be made to fly and will be reduced to dust."

Allāh ﷻ says in Sūrah Naml,

وَتَرَى الْجِبَالَ تَحْسَبُهَا جَامِدَةً وَّهِيَ تَمُرُّ مَرَّ السَّحَابِ صُنْعَ اللهِ الَّذِي أَتْقَنَ كُلَّ شَيْءٍ
إِنَّهُ خَبِيرٌ بِمَا تَفْعَلُوْنَ

"(On the Day of Judgement) you will look at the mountains thinking (expecting) them to be solid (firmly anchored in the ground) but they will be passing by like clouds (floating about in the air and eventually reduced to dust)." (27:88)

In Sūrah Muzzammil, it further stresses the same point,

يَوْمَ تَرْجُفُ الْأَرْضُ وَالْجِبَالُ وَكَانَتِ الْجِبَالُ كَثِيْبًا مَّهِيْلًا

"(This punishment will take place) on the Day (of Judgement) when the earth and the mountains will shake (shiver and quake) and the mountains will be reduced to (become) a heap of dust." (73:14)

The same scenario is echoed in the verse of Sūrah Wāqiah,

إِذَا رُجَّتِ الْأَرْضُ رَجًّا. وَّبُسَّتِ الْجِبَالُ بَسًّا

"When the earth shall convulse (shaking uncontrollably) with violent earthquakes. And the mountains will be shattered (crumbled) to pieces." (56:4-5)

The Sahābah ؓ asked the Holy Prophet ﷺ regarding the mountains, which has been recorded in the Holy Qur'ān,

"They ask you (O' Rasūlullāh) about the mountains (what will happen to the mountains on the Day of Judgement). Say, 'My Lord shall completely remove them (shatter them to dust) leaving the earth as a barren (completely level) plain, on which you will neither see any depressions nor any protrusions (with nothing sunken below or standing above the ground).'"

How terrifying that Day will be when man will witness the gigantic mountains like Himalayas, Everest and K2 being reduced to dust and flying like dust particles.

Hell-Fire

إِنَّ جَهَنَّمَ كَانَتْ مِرْصَادًا. لِّلطَّاغِيْنَ مَاٰبًا. لَّابِثِيْنَ فِيْهَا أَحْقَابًا. لَا يَذُوْقُوْنَ فِيْهَا بَرْدًا وَّلَا شَرَابًا. إِلَّا حَمِيْمًا وَّغَسَّاقًا. جَزَاءً وِّفَاقًا. إِنَّهُمْ كَانُوْا لَا يَرْجُوْنَ حِسَابًا. وَّكَذَّبُوْا بِاٰيَاتِنَا كِذَّابًا. وَكُلَّ شَيْءٍ أَحْصَيْنَاهُ كِتَابًا. فَذُوْقُوْا فَلَنْ نَّزِيْدَكُمْ إِلَّا عَذَابًا.

21) Indeed Jahannam is a place of ambush.

22) An abode for the rebellious.

23) They will remain there for an extremely long period of time.

24) In Jahannam they will taste neither any coolness nor any drink.

25) Except boiling water and pus.

26) As a befitting punishment (for their sins).

27) Indeed they never looked forward to reckoning.

28) And adamantly falsified Our verses.

29) We have meticulously recorded everything in the book.

30) So taste! We shall increase you only in punishment.

"Indeed, Jahannam is a place of ambush."

From verse 21 to verse 30, Allāh ﷻ mentions the plight of the disbeliev-ers and polytheists. The angels appointed to punish people in Jahannam are lying in wait for them. No sooner will they arrive that the angels will start punishing them. Some commentators state that the verse should be translated as, **"Indeed, Jahannam is waiting in ambush."** Lending the description to Jahannam itself is not farfetched because Allāh ﷻ has giv-en life to Jahannam.

Allāh ﷻ says in Sūrah Furqān,

إِذَا رَأَتْهُم مِّن مَّكَانٍ بَعِيدٍ سَمِعُوا لَهَا تَغَيُّظًا وَزَفِيرًا

"When it (Jahannam) will see from a distance (on the Day of Judge-ment), (it will be so intense that) they will hear the roar of its fury and its crackling (flames)." (25:12)

In another verse Allāh ﷻ says,

يَوْمَ نَقُولُ لِجَهَنَّمَ هَلِ امْتَلَأْتِ وَتَقُولُ هَلْ مِن مَّزِيدٍ

24

**"On that Day (of Qiyāmah) We shall ask Jahannam, 'Are you full?'
And it will reply, 'Are there any more (to come because I still have
space)?'" (50:30)**

Allāh ﷻ further says that Jahannam is an abode for the rebellious. The
most rebellious are the disbelievers and the polytheists. They will remain there for an extremely long period of time. The Arabic word
'Ahqāb' (translated as an extremely long period of time) in verse 23 is
the plural of 'Hiqb.' According to Hasan Basri ◉ the word refers to an
infinite period of time. According to Sayyidunā Abdullāh Ibn Mas'ood
◉, Sayyidunā Abdullāh Ibn Umar ◉, Sayyidunā Abdullāh Ibn Abbās ◉
and Sayyidunā Abū Hurairah ◉, a single Hiqb is equivalent to 80 years.
It has also been reported that a single day of these 80 years is equal to a
thousand years in this world.

Whatever the interpretation, the Holy Qur'ān is clear that people will
spend many periods of Hiqb in Jahannam. Due to the fact that the period of 'Hiqb' has not been specified and also because Sūrah Nisa and
Sūrah Jinn mention the word 'Abada' (until eternity) when mentioning
the punishment of the disbelievers and polytheists, it is the belief of the
Ahlus-Sunnah Wal Jamā'at that the disbelievers and the polytheists will
suffer eternally in Jahannam, just as the believers will enjoy Jannah eternally. Just as the bounties of the people of Jannah will never come to an
end, the punishment of the people in Jahannam will also not come to an
end. It is for this reason that commentators state that the interpretation
of Ahqāb is Hiqb after Hiqb, i.e. the people of Jahannam will suffer Hiqb
after Hiqb of punishment until eternity.

In Sūrah Nisā, Allāh ﷻ states,

$$ أُولَٰئِكَ مَأْوَاهُمْ جَهَنَّمُ وَلَا يَجِدُونَ عَنْهَا مَحِيصًا $$

25

"The abode of these people is Jahannam and they will not find an escape from it." (4:121)

In another verse of Sūrah Nisā, it says,

إِنَّ الَّذِيْنَ كَفَرُوْا وَظَلَمُوْا لَمْ يَكُنِ اللهُ لِيَغْفِرَ لَهُمْ وَلَا لِيَهْدِيَهُمْ طَرِيْقًا . إِلَّا طَرِيْقَ
جَهَنَّمَ خَالِدِيْنَ فِيْهَا أَبَدًا وَكَانَ ذٰلِكَ عَلَى اللهِ يَسِيْرًا

"Indeed, those who commit disbelief and oppress (hide the truth), Allāh will never forgive them nor guide them to any path except to the path of (leading to) Jahannam, where they shall live forever. This is ever so easy for Allāh." (4:168-169)

In Sūrah Jinn, He states,

وَمَنْ يَّعْصِ اللهَ وَرَسُوْلَهُ فَإِنَّ لَهُ نَارَ جَهَنَّمَ خَالِدِيْنَ فِيْهَا أَبَدًا

"Whoever disobeys Allāh and His Messenger shall have the Fire of Jahannam where they will live (in misery) forever." (72:23)

Allāh ﷻ continues, **"In Jahannam they will have neither any coolness nor any drink."** The people of Jahannam will have no respite from punishment, neither will they have relief from the heat nor from thirst. Of course, this verse does not contradict the existence of 'Zamhareer' - an icy cold part of Jahannam in which many people will be placed for punishment. The coolness mentioned in this verse refers to a welcome relief from the heat of Jahannam and not an icy cold punishment.

Allāh ﷻ then adds that the only drink the people of Jahannam will receive will be boiling water and pus.
Allāh ﷻ says in Sūrah Muhammad,

وَسُقُوۡا مَآءً حَمِيۡمًا فَقَطَّعَ أَمۡعَآءَهُمۡ

"They (the people of Jahannam) are given boiling water to drink which tears (pulls down) their internal organs to shreds." (47:15)

In Sūrah Wāqiah, it says:

فَشَارِبُوۡنَ شُرۡبَ الۡهِيۡمِ

"You shall (then) drink boiling water (upon it to try to force the scraps of Zaqqoom tree down) like thirsty camels." (56:55)

In Sūrah An'ām it says:

لَهُمۡ شَرَابٌ مِّنۡ حَمِيۡمٍ وَّعَذَابٌ أَلِيۡمٌ بِمَا كَانُوۡا يَكۡفُرُوۡنَ

"They (the disbelievers) shall have a drink of boiling water and an unbearable punishment because they used to commit disbelief." (6:70)

The Holy Prophet ﷺ said that if a single bucket of Ghassāq (pus) was to be thrown on earth, every person on earth would rot. (Mishkāt)

In Mirqāt, the famous commentary of Mishkāt, four interpretations of 'Ghassāq' have been cited:

1) It is the pus of the people of Jahannam and the fluid that remains after their wounds are washed.
2) It is the tears of the people in Jahannam.
3) It refers to Zamhareer which is the icy cold part of Jahannam.
4) It is the frozen, decaying puss of the people in Jahannam which is too cold to drink (however, people will be forced to drink it because of ex-

treme thirst).

Allāh ﷻ then says that whatever the people of Jahannam will suffer shall be a befitting punishment for their sins. Due to the fact that Kufr (disbelief) and Shirk (polytheism) are the worst of sins, the disbelievers and polytheists deserve the worst of punishment. They will suffer punishment for eternity because they lived their entire lives as disbelievers and polytheists.

Regarding Shirk, Allāh ﷻ categorically pronounces in different verses of the Holy Qur'ān that it will never be forgiven.

In Sūrah Nisa, verse 116, Allāh ﷻ says,

إِنَّ اللّٰهَ لَا يَغْفِرُ أَن يُّشْرَكَ بِهٖ وَيَغْفِرُ مَا دُوْنَ ذٰلِكَ لِمَنْ يَّشَاءُ وَمَنْ يُّشْرِكْ بِاللّٰهِ فَقَدِ افْتَرٰى إِثْمًا عَظِيْمًا

"Verily, Allāh shall not forgive that Shirk be committed but will forgive all sins besides this for whom He wills. Whoever ascribes partners to Allāh (commits Shirk) has indeed invented a terrible sin." (4:48)

Sayyidunā Luqmān عليه السلام advising his son, says,

يَا بُنَيَّ لَا تُشْرِكْ بِاللّٰهِ إِنَّ الشِّرْكَ لَظُلْمٌ عَظِيْمٌ

"O' my beloved son! Do not ascribe partners to Allāh. Without doubt Shirk is worst injustice (because it equates unworthy beings with Allāh)." (31:13)

Allāh ﷻ, then says about these people, **"Indeed, they never looked forward to reckoning and adamantly falsified Our verses."**

The disbelievers thought that there are no accounts or reckoning after death, hence, they occupied themselves in the luxuries and comfort of this world. When reminded, they used to say,

مَا هِيَ إِلَّا حَيَاتُنَا الدُّنْيَا نَمُوْتُ وَنَحْيَا وَمَا يُهْلِكُنَا إِلَّا الدَّهْرُ

"This is nothing but our worldly life (after which there will be no other life). We live and die and it is only time that will destroy us (we die because our bodily functions deteriorate with age)." (45:24)

Explaining their condition, Allāh ﷻ says in Sūrah Yūnus, verse 7,

إِنَّ الَّذِيْنَ لَا يَرْجُوْنَ لِقَآءَنَا وَرَضُوْا بِالْحَيَاةِ الدُّنْيَا وَاطْمَأَنُّوْا بِهَا وَالَّذِيْنَ هُمْ عَنْ آيَاتِنَا غَافِلُوْنَ أُولَٰئِكَ مَأْوَاهُمُ النَّارُ بِمَا كَانُوْا يَكْسِبُوْنَ

"Indeed, those who do not wish to meet Us, who are pleased and contented with the life of the world (because they do not believe in the Hereafter and have no concern for the Hereafter) and who are indifferent towards Our Signs, these are the ones whose abode (final resting place) shall be the Fire (of Jahannam) because of what they earn (because of their incorrect beliefs and sins)." (10:07)

No one will be able to deny their wrong doings because Allāh ﷻ says, **"We have meticulously recorded everything in the book."**

In Sūrah Yāseen, this point is made even more crystal clear, He says,

إِنَّا نَحْنُ نُحْيِ الْمَوْتَى وَنَكْتُبُ مَا قَدَّمُوْا وَآثَارَهُمْ وَكُلَّ شَيْءٍ أَحْصَيْنَاهُ فِيْ إِمَامٍ مُّبِيْنٍ

"Verily, only We (can) revive the deed and record what (actions) they send ahead (to be rewarded or punished in the Hereafter) and the trails

(guidance) which they leave behind for others to follow. We have meticulously recorded everything in the clear book (Lawhul-
Mahfooz)." (36:12)

Allāh ﷻ concludes the Ruku by stating, **"So taste (the punishment); We
shall increase you only in punishment."**

In Sūrah Nahl, He says,

الَّذِينَ كَفَرُوا وَصَدُّوا عَن سَبِيلِ اللّٰهِ زِدْنَاهُمْ عَذَابًا فَوْقَ الْعَذَابِ بِمَا كَانُوا يُفْسِدُونَ

**"For those who commit kufr (disbelief) and who prevent (others) from
Allāh's path, We shall add punishment to their punishment because of
the corruption that they caused (together with suffering for their own
wrongdoing, they will also suffer for the wrongdoing of those whom
they encouraged to do wrong)." (16:88)**

Bounties of Paradise

إِنَّ لِلْمُتَّقِينَ مَفَازًا . حَدَائِقَ وَأَعْنَابًا . وَّكَوَاعِبَ أَتْرَابًا . وَّكَأْسًا دِهَاقًا . لَا يَسْمَعُونَ
فِيهَا لَغْوًا وَّلَا كِذَّابًا . جَزَاءً مِّن رَّبِّكَ عَطَاءً حِسَابًا . رَّبِّ السَّمَاوَاتِ وَالْأَرْضِ وَمَا
بَيْنَهُمَا الرَّحْمٰنِ لَا يَمْلِكُونَ مِنْهُ خِطَابًا

31) Those with piety shall certainly have success.
32) Gardens and grapes.
33) And youthful maidens of equal age.
34) And brimming glasses.
35) In (Jannah) they shall hear neither futile talk nor lies.
36) (All this will be) Compensation, conferred as an ample gift from
your Lord.

37) Who is the Lord of the heavens, the earth and whatever is between them, the Most Compassionate. They will be unable to address Him.

After speaking about the terrible plight that the disbelievers will suffer in the Hereafter, Allāh ﷻ discusses the good fortune of those who possess Taqwa (piety). There are various levels of Taqwa. The first level is abstaining from Shirk.

The Kalimah Shahādah is referred to as Kalimah - Taqwa, as mentioned in Sūrah Fath,

"Allāh sent His tranquillity (patience) to the heart of His Messenger and to the hearts of the believers and stuck the word of Taqwa (the Kalimah) unto them as they are most deserving of it and worthy of it." (48:26)

Scholars have mentioned 5 different levels of Taqwa:
1) Abstaining from Shirk and Kufr as mentioned.
2) Abstaining from Al-Kabāir (major sins) as mentioned in the Qur'anic verse,

إِن تَجْتَنِبُوا كَبَائِرَ مَا تُنْهَوْنَ عَنْهُ نُكَفِّرْ عَنكُمْ سَيِّئَاتِكُمْ وَنُدْخِلْكُم مُّدْخَلًا كَرِيمًا

"If you avoid the major sins that you are forbidden from (those sins for which a punishment, penalty or curse have been mentioned), We shall wipe out (forgive) your evil actions (minor sins) and enter you into a place of honour (Jannah)." (4:31)

3) Abstaining from minor sins.
4) Abstaining from doubtful matters as mentioned in the famous Hadeeth,

دَعْ مَا يُرِيْبُكَ إِلَى مَا لَا يُرِيْبُكَ

"Leave that which puts you in doubt for that which does not put you in doubt." (Nasai, Tirmizi)

Likewise, the Hadeeth,

اَلْحَلَالُ بَيِّنٌ، وَالْحَرَامُ بَيِّنٌ، وَبَيْنَهُمَا أُمُوْرٌ مُشْتَبِهَةٌ

"Halāl is clear and Harām is clear. And in between them, there are doubtful matters."(Bukhāri)

5) Abstain from even those matters which are apparently permissible, lest a person transgresses towards doubtful or sinful acts.

According to the levels of Taqwa, a person will enjoy varied levels in Jannah. In the eyes of Allāh ﷻ, Taqwa is the criterion for a person's success rate. As mentioned in Sūrah Hujurāt,

إِنَّ أَكْرَمَكُمْ عِنْدَ اللهِ أَتْقَاكُمْ إِنَّ اللهَ عَلِيْمٌ خَبِيْرٌ

"Verily, the most honoured of you in the sight of Allāh is the one with the most Taqwa (piety and righteousness). Allāh is certainly All-Knowing, Informed (only He knows whose Taqwa is best)." (49:13)

Allāh ﷻ says,

إِنَّ لِلْمُتَّقِيْنَ مَفَازًا

"Those with Taqwa shall certainly have success." (78:31)

Although the word مَفَازًا (Mafāza) is translated as success, it also refers to a place of success i.e. Jannah. 'Mafāza' here is Ism Zarf (a noun denoting to a place), therefore it means a place of success. Allāh ﷻ then recounts the bounties of Jannah which are a manifestation of a person's success. These bounties include gardens. The Arabic word used for gardens is 'Hadā'iq' which is the plural of 'Hadeeqa.' Hadeeqa actually refers to a garden or an orchard that is surrounded by four walls. Although grapes are to be found in such orchards like all other fruits, Allāh ﷻ mentions grapes separately because grapes are a more celebrated fruit than other fruits.

Also, among the bounties of Jannah will be youthful maidens of equal age so that compatibility will be optimal. Sayyidunā Abū Sa'eed Al-Khudree ؓ narrates from the Holy Prophet ﷺ that every person to enter Jannah will be thirty years of age, irrespective of their age in this world when they passed away. Therefore, they will not age.

Once, a lady came in the presence of the Holy Prophet ﷺ and asked, "O' Messenger of Allāh ﷺ, pray that Allāh ﷺ enters me into Jannah." The Holy Prophet ﷺ said to her, "Old women will not enter Jannah." Hearing this, the old woman left weeping. The Holy Prophet ﷺ sent someone after her with the message that she will not be old when she enters Jannah; she will be transformed into a young lady, because Allāh ﷻ states,

إِنَّا أَنْشَأْنَاهُنَّ إِنْشَاءً . فَجَعَلْنَاهُنَّ أَبْكَارًا . عُرُبًا أَتْرَابًا . لِّأَصْحَابِ الْيَمِينِ

"Indeed, We have created them (the damsels whom the people of the right shall marry) pure (without any impurities in their bodies or their behaviour). And We have made them all virgins. Most beloved (every facet of their appearance and behaviour will be pleasing to their husbands) and of equal age for the people of the right." (56:35-37)

Allāh ﷻ states further that in Jannah, people will enjoy brimming glasses. This verse does not contradict verse 11 of Sūrah Dahr where Allāh ﷻ says,

قَوَارِيرَ مِن فِضَّةٍ قَدَّرُوهَا تَقْدِيرًا

"Such crystal that is of silver (unlike anything of this world), with an appropriate measure." (76:16)

There is no contradiction because those people who desire to have their glasses brimming over will have their desire. For the people of Jannah, there will be so many different types of drink.

In Sūrah Dahr, describing the utensils and glasses, it says,

وَيُطَافُ عَلَيْهِم بِآنِيَةٍ مِّن فِضَّةٍ وَأَكْوَابٍ كَانَتْ قَوَارِيرَا

"Utensils of silver (containing the most sumptuous foods) will be brought to them as well as glasses of crystal (containing the most delicious drinks)." (76:15)

Further on it says,

وَيُسْقَوْنَ فِيهَا كَأْسًا كَانَ مِزَاجُهَا زَنجَبِيلًا . عَيْنًا فِيهَا تُسَمَّى سَلْسَبِيلًا

"They will be given to drink from cups containing a (wonderful) ginger like mixture. (They will drink from) A spring there (in Jannah) called Salsabeel (pure and clean water)."

In Jannah, people shall hear neither futile talk nor lies. Not only will the people of Jannah not speak lies and hold useless discussions, they will not even hear this from others. This is further explained in the verse of Sūrah Wāqiah,

لَا يَسْمَعُونَ فِيهَا لَغْوًا وَّلَا تَأْثِيمًا . إِلَّا قِيلًا سَلَامًا سَلَامًا

"They will not hear any (unpleasant) noise there (in Jannah), nor any

foolish (idle and sinful) talk. Instead they will hear the (pleasant) call of Salām (peace), (they will greet each other with the words of Salām, be greeted by the angels with these words and Allāh will also greet them with these words)." (56:25-26)

Allāh ﷻ continues,

جَزَآءً مِّن رَّبِّكَ عَطَآءً حِسَابًا

"(All this will be) compensation (for their good deeds), conferred as an ample gift from your Lord."

Whatever the people of Jannah receive will be much more than everything they desired. There will be nothing left to be desired.

Allāh ﷻ says,

"There (in Jannah), you shall have whatever your heart desires and you shall have whatever you ask for. This is the hospitality from the Most Forgiving, the Most Merciful." (41:31-32)

In Sūrah Zukhruf, it says,

وَفِيهَا مَا تَشْتَهِيهِ الْأَنْفُسُ وَتَلَذُّ الْأَعْيُنُ وَأَنْتُمْ فِيهَا خَالِدُونَ

"In Jannah there shall be whatever the heart desires and whatever pleases the eye. You shall live there forever." (43:71)

Helplessness on the Day of Judgement

رَبِّ السَّمَاوَاتِ وَالْأَرْضِ وَمَا بَيْنَهُمَا الرَّحْمَنِ

"The Lord of the heavens, the earth and whatever is between them, the Most Compassionate." (78:37)

Allāh ﷻ describes Himself by saying that He, the Lord has the sovereignty of the heavens and the earth and all that it contains.

لَا يَمْلِكُونَ مِنْهُ خِطَابًا

"Whom they will be unable to address." (78:37)

The people of Jahannam will not be able to request respite and the people of Jannah will be unable to ask for more without His permission.

On the Day of Judgement, all affairs will be solely in the control of Allāh ﷻ as mentioned in numerous verses which mention that no one will be able to intercede or help without His permission.

In Sūrah Infitār, it says,

يَوْمَ لَا تَمْلِكُ نَفْسٌ لِّنَفْسٍ شَيْئًا وَالْأَمْرُ يَوْمَئِذٍ لِّلّٰهِ

"It shall be a Day when one soul will be unable to benefit (assist) another soul in the least. On that Day, all authority will be Allāh's (and no one else will have any say in the judgement of affairs)." (82:19)

يَوْمَ يَقُومُ الرُّوحُ وَالْمَلَائِكَةُ صَفًّا لَّا يَتَكَلَّمُونَ إِلَّا مَنْ أَذِنَ لَهُ الرَّحْمَنُ وَقَالَ صَوَابًا.

ذَٰلِكَ الْيَوْمُ الْحَقُّ فَمَنْ شَآءَ اتَّخَذَ إِلَىٰ رَبِّهِ مَآبًا . إِنَّا أَنْذَرْنَاكُمْ عَذَابًا قَرِيبًا يَّوْمَ يَنْظُرُ الْمَرْءُ مَا قَدَّمَتْ يَدَاهُ وَيَقُوْلُ الْكَافِرُ يَا لَيْتَنِيْ كُنْتُ تُرَابًا .

38) On the Day when the Spirit (Jibreel and every living being) and the angels will stand in rows, none of them will be able to speak except the one whom Rahmān permits and who speaks correctly.

39) That is the Day of Truth. So whoever wills should adopt a recourse towards his Lord.

40) We have certainly warned you of a near punishment; the Day when a man will see what his hands sent ahead and the disbeliever will say, "O! If only I had been dust!"

Allāh ﷻ describes the restlessness and horror of that Day by mentioning that only those whom He grants permission to speak will speak. These people will be the ones whom Allāh ﷻ knows will speak correctly.

In Sūrah Hood, a similar verse says,

يَوْمَ يَأْتِ لَا تَكَلَّمُ نَفْسٌ إِلَّا بِإِذْنِه

"When that Day (of Qiyāmah) will dawn, a soul will only speak with Allāh's permission." (11:105)

Referring to the angels, Allāh ﷻ says in Sūrah Ambiya,

يَعْلَمُ مَا بَيْنَ أَيْدِيْهِمْ وَمَا خَلْفَهُمْ وَلَا يَشْفَعُوْنَ إِلَّا لِمَنِ ارْتَضَى وَهُمْ مِّنْ خَشْيَتِه مُشْفِقُوْنَ

"He knows what is before them and what is behind them (He knows everything they do) and only the one with whom He is pleased will be able to intercede (on behalf of anyone on the Day of Judgement) and they tremble with fear for Him." (21:28)

In Āyatul-Kursi, it says,

مَنۡ ذَا الَّذِیۡ یَشۡفَعُ عِنۡدَهٗۤ اِلَّا بِاِذۡنِه

"Who is there that can intercede before Him without His permission
(None can do this)?" (2:225)

ذٰلِكَ الۡیَوۡمُ الۡحَقُّ فَمَنۡ شَآءَ اتَّخَذَ اِلٰی رَبِّه مَاٰبًا

"That is the Day of Truth. So whoever wills should adopt a recourse
towards his Lord (i.e. one should accept Islām and continue to perform
good deeds until ones death)"

Various Names of Judgement Day

This Day has been referred to with so many different names.

یَوۡمُ الۡاٰزِفَة

1) The Day that draws ever nearer. (40:18)

یَوۡمٌ عَسِیۡرٌ

2) The Day of Anguish. (74:9)

وَالۡیَوۡمُ الۡمَوۡعُوۡدُ

3) The Promised Day. (85:2)

یَوۡمُ الۡخُلُوۡدِ

4) The Day of Eternal Life. (50:34)

38

يَوْمُ نَحْسٍ مُّسْتَمِرٍّ

5) The Day of Bitter Misfortune. (54:19)

يَوْمُ التَّغَابُنِ

6) The Day of Loss and Gain. (64:9)

الْيَوْمُ الْحَقُّ

7) The Day of Ultimate Truth. (78:39)

يَوْمُ الْحَسْرَةِ

8) The Day of Remorse (Grief and Regret). (19:39)

يَوْمٌ عَقِيْمٌ

9) The Day Void of all Hope. (22:55)

يَوْمُ الْفَتْحِ

10) The Day of the Final Decision. (32:29)

يَوْمُ الْفَصْلِ

11) The Day of Judgement. (77:14)

يَوْمُ الحِسَابِ

12) The Day of Account. (14:41)

يَوْمُ التَّلَاقِ

13) The Day Which They Shall Meet Him. (40:15)

يَوْمُ الدِّيْنِ

14) The Day of Judgement. (1:4)

يَوْمُ الْقِيَامَةِ

15) The Day of Resurrection. (2:85)

يَوْمٌ مَّجْمُوْعٌ

16) A Day When Mankind Will Be Gathered Together. (11:103)

يَوْمُ الْوَقْتِ الْمَعْلُوْمِ

17) The Day of the Appointed Time. (15:38)

اَلْغَاشِيَةُ

18) The Overwhelming Thing. (88:1)

يَوْمٌ لَّا مَرَدَّ لَهُ

19) A Day Which None Can Avert. (30:43)

لِيَوْمٍ لَّا رَيْبَ فِيْهِ

20) A Day About Which There is no Doubt. (3:9)

يَوْمٌ لَّا بَيْعٌ فِيْهِ وَلَا خُلَّةٌ

21) A Day on Which There Will be no Mutual Bargaining or Befriending. (2:254)

Allāh ﷻ concludes the Sūrah by stating,

إِنَّا أَنْذَرْنَاكُمْ عَذَابًا قَرِيْبًا

"We have certainly warned you of a near punishment."

The punishment of the Day of Judgement is near because whatever is certain is regarded as being near.

Four Questions

This reminds me of an incident where a person came to Sayyidunā Ali ؓ and said, "I want to ask you the following four questions so please reply to them.

1) What is Wājib (obligatory) and what is Awjab (most obligatory)?
2) What is Qareeb (near) and what is Aqrab (most near)?
3) What is Ajeeb (strange) and what is A'ajab (most strange)?
4) What is Sa'b (difficult) and what is As'ab (most difficult)?"

Sayyidunā Ali ؓ replied as follows,
"1) Obligatory is the obedience of Allāh ﷻ and most obligatory is to abandon sins.
2) Near is the Day of Judgement and most near is death.
3) Strange is this world and most strange is to have love for this world.
4) Difficult is the grave and most difficult is going into it without any provisions (preparations for the Hereafter)."

Plight of the Disbelievers

Allāh ﷻ continues in the last verse of the Sūrah by explaining the painful plight of man,

يَوْمَ يَنْظُرُ الْمَرْءُ مَا قَدَّمَتْ يَدَاهُ

"The Day when a man will see what (deeds) his hands sent ahead (in his record of deeds)".

Allāh ﷻ says in Sūrah Fajr,

وَجِيْءَ يَوْمَئِذٍ بِجَهَنَّمَ يَوْمَئِذٍ يَتَذَكَّرُ الْإِنْسَانُ وَأَنَّى لَهُ الذِّكْرَى. يَقُوْلُ يَا لَيْتَنِيْ قَدَّمْتُ لِحَيَاتِيْ

"And the Day when Jahannam will be brought to the front (for all to see). On that Day, man will understand (the errors of his ways in this world). But of what use will this understanding be (because it will be too late to make amends)? He (man) will say, 'Oh dear! If only I had sent (good deeds) ahead (to earn rewards) for my life (here in the Hereafter).'" (89:23-24)

In Sūrah Kahf, Allāh ﷻ says,

وَوُضِعَ الْكِتَابُ فَتَرَى الْمُجْرِمِيْنَ مُشْفِقِيْنَ مِمَّا فِيْهِ وَيَقُوْلُوْنَ يَا وَيْلَتَنَا مَالِ هٰذَا الْكِتَابِ لَا يُغَادِرُ صَغِيْرَةً وَّلَا كَبِيْرَةً إِلَّا أَحْصَاهَا وَوَجَدُوْا مَا عَمِلُوْا حَاضِرًا وَلَا يَظْلِمُ رَبُّكَ أَحَدًا

"The book (every person's record of actions) shall be placed (given to them) and you will see the sinners (those whose records will be given

42

in their left hands) afraid of what is contained in them (because it will condemn them to Jahannam). They will say, 'We are destroyed! What kind of book is this? (It is so thorough that) it does not leave anything (any action) small or large unrecorded? They will find their actions (which they carried out in the world) present (written in their records) and your Lord shall not oppress anyone (no one will be punished for a sin one did not commit nor deprived of reward for a good act carried out)." (18:49)

In Sūrah Zilzāl, Allāh ﷻ says,

$$فَمَنْ يَّعْمَلْ مِثْقَالَ ذَرَّةٍ خَيْرًا يَّرَهُ . وَمَنْ يَّعْمَلْ مِثْقَالَ ذَرَّةٍ شَرًّا يَّرَهُ$$

"Whoever has (sincerely) done an atom's weight of good, will see it (the consequences when he is rewarded for it) and whoever has done an atom's weight of evil (without securing Allāh's forgiveness for it), will see it (the consequences when he is punished for it)." (99:7-8)

Allāh ﷻ concludes by stating,

$$وَيَقُوْلُ الْكَافِرُ يَا لَيْتَنِيْ كُنْتُ تُرَابًا$$

"The disbeliever will say, 'Oh! If only I had been dust!'"

It is reported from Sayyidunā Abdullāh Ibn Umar ؓ that every creature will be resurrected on the Day of Judgement, even the birds and animals. Then, retribution will be taken from every one of them who oppressed another in any way. Consequently, a hornless goat will have revenge from the horned goat that butted it in the world. When revenge is taken from all the animals, Allāh ﷻ will command them, "Become dust!"

Seeing this, the disbeliever will think that it would have been better for

43

him if he was an animal so that his affair would be terminated after revenge is taken. He would then not have to suffer any further punishment. Although animals will have no reward they will also have no punishment. It is on this occasion that the disbeliever will say, **"Oh! If only I
had been dust!"**

**Alhamdulillāh, the commentary of Sūrah Naba has been completed at
11:20am on Friday 15ᵗʰ November 2013 (11ᵗʰ of Muharram 1435) before
Jumu'ah. May Allāh ﷻ accept it from His humble and sinful servant.
Āmeen!**

Sūrah Nāzi'āt

Those Who Extract
Revealed in Makkah

بِسْمِ اللهِ الرَّحْمٰنِ الرَّحِيْمِ

In the name of Allāh, the Most Compassionate, the Most Merciful.

وَالنَّازِعَاتِ غَرْقًا . وَّالنَّاشِطَاتِ نَشْطًا . وَّالسَّابِحَاتِ سَبْحًا . فَالسَّابِقَاتِ سَبْقًا .

فَالْمُدَبِّرَاتِ أَمْرًا

1) By the oath of those angels who harshly extract (tear out the souls of the disbelievers).

2) (And) those (angels) who (draw out the souls of the believers as gently as they) untie knots.

3) And those who (speedily take the souls of the dead to the heavens as if they) are swimming along.

4) And those who swiftly race (along with the souls after Allāh instructs them whether the soul should be rewarded among the righteous or punished with the disbelievers and sinners).

5) And (by the oath of) those (angels) who arrange (to carry out) the commands (of Allāh).

In the Holy Qur'ān, there are five Sūrahs which have a similar beginning. One of them being this particular Sūrah Nāzi'āt. The second is Sūrah Sāffāt, the third is Sūrah Zāriyāt, the fourth is Sūrah Mursalāt and the fifth is Sūrah Ādiyāt.

In Sūrah Sāffāt, three attributes are mentioned with the oath, in Sūrah Zāriyāt, four qualities are mentioned and in the remaining three, five qualities are mentioned with the oath.

45

"By the oath of those angels who harshly extract."

Allāh ﷻ begins the Sūrah by taking oaths of several types of Angels to assert that the Day (shall certainly take place) when that which shakes shall shake.

The oath of the angels is apt on this occasion because they are always involved in the administration and running of the world. They are executing their duties loyally, as mentioned very clearly in the verses of the Holy Qur'ān.

لَا يَعْصُونَ اللّٰهَ مَا أَمَرَهُمْ وَيَفْعَلُونَ مَا يُؤْمَرُونَ

"They (the angels) never disobey what Allāh commands them and they carry out exactly what they are instructed (to do)." (66:06)

لَا يَسْبِقُونَهُ بِالْقَوْلِ وَهُمْ بِأَمْرِهِ يَعْمَلُونَ

"They (the angels) do not speak before Him and they carry out His orders (in complete submission)." (21:27)

Five characteristics of the angels are mentioned which are connected with or related to the extraction of the soul at the time of death.

First Characteristic

وَالنَّازِعَاتِ غَرْقًا

"By the oath of those (angels) who harshly extract souls."

This refers to the angels of punishment who extract the souls of the disbelievers vigorously and harshly. The word harshly refers to spiritual pain. The people around the dying person may not be sensitive to the pain. Often, it is noticed that the soul of a disbeliever apparently slips out

46

easily, but the ease is only perceived by the people around the dying person. The real pain is felt by the soul of the dying person.

Second Characteristic

وَالنَّاشِطَاتِ نَشْطًا

"And those who untie knots."

The word 'Nāshitāt' is derived from 'Nasht' and it means to untie the knot. This signifies to untying the knot of something which contains water or air so that it may be released easily. This is a method for drawing out the souls of the believers gently, unlike souls of the disbelievers which are extracted harshly. In this case too, the adverb 'Nashtā' (smoothly) refers to the spiritual ease and smoothness, and not to the physical experience. Sometimes, it happens that there is a delay at the time of death of a righteous believer or an apparent hardship. This should not be taken to mean that he is undergoing some sort of suffering, although physically, it may seem so.

When the soul of a disbeliever is extracted, the entire scene of the punishment of Barzakh comes in front of him. The soul is frightened by it so it disperses throughout the body and tries to hide or escape. The angels forcefully extract the soul just as wet wool wrapped around a skewer is forcefully removed. When the soul of a believer is extracted, on the other hand, the reward, blessings and welcome news at the Barzakh come in front of him.

47

Third Characteristic

وَالسَّابِحَاتِ سَبْحًا

"And those who swim along."

The word, 'Sabh' literally means to swim or float. Here, it signifies to gliding along swiftly, as in the sea where there is no mountain barrier. The angels who float and swim swiftly refer to the quality of the angels of death who extract human souls and take them quickly towards the heavens.

Fourth Characteristic

فَالسَّابِقَاتِ سَبْقًا

"And those who swiftly race."

According to Divine instruction, the angels do not delay in transporting the souls of people to their good or bad abodes. The soul of the believer is transported to the blessings of Paradise and that of a disbeliever is transported to the torment of Hell.

Fifth Characteristic

فَالْمُدَبِّرَاتِ أَمْرًا

"And those who arrange the commands."

In other words, the last task of these angels of death will be that those who are commanded to reward and comfort the deserving souls, will gather means of reward and comfort for them; and those who are commanded to punish and cause pain (to the evil souls), will organise means for that.

يَوْمَ تَرْجُفُ الرَّاجِفَةُ . تَتْبَعُهَا الرَّادِفَةُ . قُلُوبٌ يَّوْمَئِنٍ وَّاجِفَةٌ . أَبْصَارُهَا خَاشِعَةٌ

6) That Day (of Qiyāmah shall certainly take place) when that which shakes (things) (the first blowing of the trumpet) shall (cause them to) shake and collapse.

7) To be followed by that (the second blowing of the trumpet) which will follow. (After the first blowing of the trumpet causes everything to perish, the second blowing will bring creation back to life for reckoning).

8) On that Day, many hearts will be fluttering (throbbing with fear and worry).

9) Their gazes will be cast down (in embarrassment due to what they did in the world and in humility before Allāh).

Day of Judgement

The above oaths are taken to assert that the Day of Judgement shall certainly take place. **"That which shakes,"** refers to the first blowing of the trumpet which will violently shake everything. The first blowing of the trumpet will be followed by that which will follow i.e. by the second blowing of the trumpet. In between the two blowings, there will be a duration of forty years. Describing the condition of people on the Day of Judgement, Allāh ﷻ says, **"On that Day, many hearts will be fluttering with their gazes cast down."**

In another verse He says,

فَأَمَّا الَّذِينَ اسْوَدَّتْ وُجُوهُهُمْ أَكَفَرْتُمْ بَعْدَ إِيْمَانِكُمْ فَذُوقُوا الْعَذَابَ بِمَا كُنْتُمْ تَكْفُرُوْنَ

"As for those whose faces shall be gloomy (depressed and scared because of their Kufr and hypocrisy) (it will be said to them to reprimand

them), 'Did you commit Kufr after having Imān? So taste the punishment because you committed Kufr.'" (3:106)

In Sūrah Abas, Allāh ﷻ says,

"And (on the other hand) many faces will be dusty, covered with darkness. These will be the sinful disbelievers." (80:41-42)

يَقُولُونَ أَإِنَّا لَمَرْدُودُونَ فِي الْحَافِرَةِ . أَإِذَا كُنَّا عِظَامًا نَّخِرَةً . قَالُوا تِلْكَ إِذًا كَرَّةٌ خَاسِرَةٌ . فَإِنَّمَا هِيَ زَجْرَةٌ وَّاحِدَةٌ . فَإِذَا هُم بِالسَّاهِرَةِ

10) They (the disbelievers) say, "Will we be returned to our former states (will we be raised up on the Day of Judgement)?
11) "Even after we have (died and) become decayed bones?"
12) They (sarcastically) say, "This (if we are resurrected), shall be a tremendous loss (to us because we have not prepared)."
13) It will only be a single blast (of the trumpet to signal the arrival of Qiyāmah).
14) And they will all suddenly be awakened (from their graves to present themselves for reckoning).

Allāh ﷻ then quotes what the disbelievers used to say about the Day of Judgement. They will say, **"Will we be returned to our former states even after we have become decomposed bones?"** The disbelievers regard the advent of Qiyāmah as something farfetched and cynically ask this question.

Allāh ﷻ also quotes this saying in Sūrah Yaseen . He says,

قَالَ مَنْ يُّحْيِ الْعِظَامَ وَهِيَ رَمِيمٌ

"Who will give life to (revive the) bones after they have decomposed (decayed)." (36:78)

In the next verse, Allāh ﷻ answers their sarcastic question by stating, **"Say (O' Prophet Muhammad), the One Who gave life to it the first time (when He first created it) will revive it. He has knowledge of all things." (36:79)**

The disbelievers also say, **"This (the return) shall be a tremendous loss."** The disbelievers said that if Qiyāmah was to take place as the Holy Prophet ﷺ said, they would be ruined because they will suffer the punishment for their rejection. However, this statement was intended to mock the belief of Qiyāmah because the disbelievers did not even vaguely believe that Qiyāmah could be reality. If they had the concern that they may have to suffer a loss, they would not have behaved as badly as they did.

For the disbelievers, the worldly life was everything.

وَقَالُوا مَا هِيَ إِلَّا حَيَاتُنَا الدُّنْيَا نَمُوتُ وَنَحْيَا وَمَا يُهْلِكُنَا إِلَّا الدَّهْرُ

"They (the disbelievers) say, 'This is nothing but our worldly life (after which there will be no other life). We die and we live and it is only time that will destroy us (we die only because our bodily functions deteriorate with age).'" (45:24)

"It will be only a single blast and they will all suddenly be awakened (to present themselves for reckoning)." Although the disbelievers regarded the advent of Qiyāmah to be something farfetched and impossible, it is an extremely simple matter for Allāh ﷻ. When Allāh ﷻ gives the command, all it takes for the people to be resurrected for Qiyāmah is a single blast of the trumpet and everyone will present themselves without delay.

In Sūrah Qiyāmah, Allāh ﷻ quotes the saying of the disbelievers,

يَسْأَلُ أَيَّانَ يَوْمُ الْقِيَامَةِ

"He (sarcastically) asks, 'When will the Day of Qiyāmah come?'" (75:06)

Allāh ﷻ answers in the next few verses. **"When eyes will be bewildered (dazed out of extreme fear), the moon will eclipse (lose its light) and the sun and moon will be joined (and both will be without light). Man will say on that Day, 'Where is an escape?' 'No! There is definitely no place of safety (to escape) on this Day; the only abode (place of safety) shall be towards your Lord.' On that Day, man will be informed of whatever (actions) he had sent ahead (carried out) and left behind (in the world without carrying out).'"**

فَإِذَا هُمْ بِالسَّاهِرَةِ

"And they will all suddenly be awakened (to present themselves for reckoning)."

The word 'Sāhira' refers to the surface of the earth. When the earth will be re-created at the time of resurrection, it will be a completely level surface. There will be no mountains, barriers, buildings or caves.

How beautifully Allāh ﷻ describes this in the verse of Sūrah Tāhā, **"They ask you (O Prophet of Allāh) about the mountains (what will happen to the mountains on the Day of Qiyāmah). Say, 'My Lord shall completely remove them (shatter them to dust) leaving the earth as a barren (completely level) plain, on which you will neither see any depres-**

sions nor any protrusions (with nothing sunken below nor standing above the ground).'"

The word, 'Sāhira' comes from the root word سهر (Sahara) which means to remain awake. It is referred to as 'Sāhira' in this context to explain that there will be no rest or sleep due to the fear and grief of the Day of Resurrection.

Story of Sayyidunā Moosā عليه السلام

هَلْ أَتَاكَ حَدِيْثُ مُوْسَى . إِذْ نَادَاهُ رَبُّهُ بِالْوَادِ الْمُقَدَّسِ طُوًى . اذْهَبْ إِلَى فِرْعَوْنَ إِنَّهُ طَغَى . فَقُلْ هَلْ لَّكَ إِلَى أَنْ تَزَكَّى . وَأَهْدِيَكَ إِلَى رَبِّكَ فَتَخْشَى . فَأَرَاهُ الْآيَةَ الْكُبْرَى . فَكَذَّبَ وَعَصَى . ثُمَّ أَدْبَرَ يَسْعَى . فَحَشَرَ فَنَادَى . فَقَالَ أَنَا رَبُّكُمُ الْأَعْلَى . فَأَخَذَهُ اللّٰهُ نَكَالَ الْآخِرَةِ وَالْأُوْلَى . إِنَّ فِيْ ذٰلِكَ لَعِبْرَةً لِّمَنْ يَّخْشَى .

15) Has the story of Moosā reached you?
16) (Remember the time) when his Lord called him in the Holy Valley of Tuwā (and commanded him to take the message of Tawheed to Fir'awn and his people).
17) (Allāh said to Moosā) "Go to (preach Tawheed to) Fir'awn for he has certainly transgressed (has become rebellious).
18) Then say, 'Do you want to be purified (from Kufr and sin)?
19) And should I guide you to your Lord so that you may fear Him?)'"
20) So he (Moosā) showed him (Fir'awn) a great sign (many miracles).
21) But he (Fir'awn) rejected (the message) and disobeyed)the commands of Allāh that Moosā conveyed to him).
22) Then he turned back and applied himself (plotted to defeat Moosā).

23) Then he gathered (the people) and announced.

24) He said, "I am your highest Lord."

25) So (because of his rebellion) Allāh seized him with the punishment of the Ākhirah (Jahannam) and the world (drowning).

26) There is certainly a lesson (to ponder over) in this for the one who fears (Allāh's punishment).

هَلْ أَتَاكَ حَدِيْثُ مُوْسَى

"Has the story of Moosā reached you?"

The objective of mentioning the story of Sayyidunā Moosā عليه السلام was to console the Holy Prophet ﷺ and at the same time, to warn and reprimand his people from opposing him. It is as though Allāh ﷻ is addressing him, "O' My beloved, remain patient like Prophet Moosā عليه السلام. Indeed, your people, even though they have transgressed in disbelief, have not reached the limits of Fir'awn. Indeed, Allāh ﷻ punished and destroyed Fir'awn and his large army even though he was much mightier in power and status than your people. Ultimately, the disbelievers will face a humiliating punishment."

The story of Sayyidunā Moosā عليه السلام is discussed in many Sūrahs of the Holy Qur'ān. The connection and relevance of mentioning the story of Sayyidunā Moosā عليه السلام after relating the condition of the disbelievers who denied resurrection is quite marvellous. A thought might come across a believer's mind that why does Allāh ﷻ not just revive a dead person and demonstrate to the deniers of resurrection that it is all possible; the disbeliever would then have no ground to stand on. In mentioning the miracle of Sayyidunā Moosā's عليه السلام staff turning to a serpent, Allāh ﷻ answers this in a very subtle way. If the disbelievers, especially Fir'awn, did not accept a lifeless dry stick transforming into a live gigantic and active serpent, then the disbelievers of your era will not accept Imān in resurrecting a dead person. Furthermore, it is the way of Allāh ﷻ that after a clear miracle is shown and if disbelievers do not believe, then the immediate wrath of Allāh ﷻ descends upon them. Hence, it is in their favour not to show these miracles.

Coming back to the story of Sayyidunā Moosā ﷺ, I will briefly mention its background so we can grasp the understanding of the forthcoming verses. Sayyidunā Moosā ﷺ was from Banoo Isrā'eel, who lived in Egypt from the time of Sayyidunā Yūsuf ﷺ. The people of Egypt under the command of their leader, Firawn, greatly oppressed the Banoo Isrā'eel and made their lives miserable. They would kill their sons and leave their daughters to live. It was during these times that Sayyidunā Moosā ﷺ was born. Upon direction from Allāh ﷻ his mother placed him in a basket which she put in the river in order to prevent him being killed. When the basket passed by Fir'awn's palace, his wife had it removed from the river. When she saw the child inside, she was overwhelmed with love and she beseeched Fir'awn to keep the child as a son in the palace. Consequently, Sayyidunā Moosā ﷺ grew up in Fir'awn's palace.

When he grew up, he killed a Copt (a person from Fir'awn's clan) by mistake whilst trying to assist an Isrā'eeli. When the news of this reached Fir'awn and his ministers, they decided to execute Sayyidunā Moosā ﷺ. Learning of their intentions, Sayyidunā Moosā ﷺ left Egypt and settled in Madyan where he married and tended the goats of his father in law for ten years. He then decided to return to Egypt with his wife but lost the way. Eventually, he saw what appeared to be a fire in the distance. Thinking that he could get a brand of fire to keep his wife warm and find someone to direct him, Sayyidunā Moosā ﷺ set out in the direction of the 'fire.' When he reached the sacred valley of Tuwā where the 'fire' was, Allāh ﷻ addressed him and made him a Prophet. Allāh ﷻ asked him to throw down his staff, which He made into a snake. Allāh ﷻ also showed him that his hand could become a shining lamp by placing it beneath his arm. Then Allāh ﷻ commanded him to preach to Fir'awn and his people. It is with reference to this that Allāh ﷻ says, **"Has the story of Moosā reached you? When his Lord called him on the blessed valley of Tuwā, 'Go to Fir'awn, for he has certainly transgressed. Tell him, 'Do you want to be purified? And should I guide you to your Lord so that you may fear (Him)?'"**

Complying with Allāh's ﷻ command, Sayyidunā Moosā ﷺ left for Egypt where he was joined by his brother Sayyidunā Hāroon ﷺ whom Allāh ﷻ had also made a Prophet at Sayyidunā Moosā's ﷺ request. Entering Fir'awns court, they warned him about Allāh's ﷻ punishment if he did not desist from his evil ways. They told him, **"It has been revealed to us that punishment shall be for those who falsify and turn away."** Hearing that Sayyidunā Moosā ﷺ preached the Divinity of Allāh ﷻ, Fir'awn was extremely upset because he indoctrinated the people into believing that he was their God. He asked Sayyidunā Moosā ﷺ a series of questions to intimidate him, but Sayyidunā Moosā ﷺ answered all his questions with great courage. Unable to win any ground from Sayyidunā Moosā ﷺ, Fir'awn finally said, "If you take another as a deity besides myself, I shall definitely make you of the prisoners!"

قَالَ أَوَلَوْ جِئْتُكَ بِشَيْءٍ مُّبِيْنٍ . قَالَ فَأْتِ بِهِ إِنْ كُنْتَ مِنَ الصَّادِقِيْنَ . فَأَلْقَى عَصَاهُ فَإِذَا هِيَ ثُعْبَانٌ مُّبِيْنٌ . وَنَزَعَ يَدَهُ فَإِذَا هِيَ بَيْضَاءُ لِلنَّاظِرِيْنَ

"Moosā said, 'Even if I bring you a clear proof?'"
Fir'awn said, 'Bring it if you are truthful.'
So Moosā cast down his staff and it suddenly became a clear serpent. And he withdrew his hand which suddenly turned white for all to see." (26:29-33)

It is with reference to these miracles that Allāh ﷻ says, **"So he (Sayyidunā Moosā) showed him (Fir'awn) a great sign."** However, instead of accepting, Fir'awn **"falsified and disobeyed."** Fir'awn then declared that Sayyidunā Moosā عليه السلام was a magician and arranged a contest between Sayyidunā Moosā عليه السلام and the magicians of the land. Not only did Sayyidunā Moosā عليه السلام defeat the magicians, but he made them all Mu'mineen (believers).

However, Fir'awn was still adamant not to accept and continued claiming his divinity. Allāh ﷻ says that Fir'awn turned away and strived to find a way to stop the spread of Sayyidunā Moosā's عليه السلام message. He gathered the people and proclaimed, **"I am your highest Lord!"** However, all his schemes failed and he was eventually drowned with his entire army. Allāh ﷻ says, **"So Allāh seized him with the punishment of this world and the Hereafter."**

In Sūrah Yūnus, Allāh ﷻ says,

وَجَاوَزْنَا بِبَنِيْ إِسْرَآئِيْلَ الْبَحْرَ فَأَتْبَعَهُمْ فِرْعَوْنُ وَجُنُوْدُهُ بَغْيًا وَّعَدْوًا ۖ حَتّٰى إِذَآ أَدْرَكَهُ الْغَرَقُ قَالَ آمَنْتُ أَنَّهُ لَآ إِلٰهَ إِلَّا الَّذِيْ آمَنَتْ بِهِ بَنُوْ إِسْرَآئِيْلَ وَأَنَا مِنَ الْمُسْلِمِيْنَ ۔ آلْآنَ وَقَدْ عَصَيْتَ قَبْلُ وَكُنْتَ مِنَ الْمُفْسِدِيْنَ ۔ فَالْيَوْمَ نُنَجِّيْكَ بِبَدَنِكَ لِتَكُوْنَ لِمَنْ خَلْفَكَ آيَةً ۚ وَإِنَّ كَثِيْرًا مِّنَ النَّاسِ عَنْ آيَاتِنَا لَغَافِلُوْنَ

"(After escaping from Egypt) We made the Banoo Isrā'eel cross the sea (Red Sea) while Fir'awn and his army (doggedly) chased them out of defiance and tyranny. (They continued to give chase and even entered the pathways Allāh created for Banoo Isrā'eel in the sea) until (the time came when the pathways in the sea closed and) Fir'awn began to drown, he said, 'I believe that there is no deity but Him in whom the

57

Banoo Isrā'eel believe and I am from those who surrender.'
(It was then said to him, 'Do you believe only) now when (all the
while) you were disobedient before (this incident that is claiming
your life) and you were among those who caused corruption (by mis-
leading and oppressing others)?' (He was further told) 'Today, We
shall preserve (save) you with your body to be a sign (and a lesson) for
those after you (people who choose your course)'. (Unfortunately) there
are certainly many people who are negligent of Our Signs (and fail to
learn lessons from them)." (10:90-92)

In Sūrah Hūd, Allāh ﷻ says,

يَقْدُمُ قَوْمَهُ يَوْمَ الْقِيَامَةِ فَأَوْرَدَهُمُ النَّارَ وَبِئْسَ الْوِرْدُ الْمَوْرُوْدُ

"He will lead his people on the Day of Judgement and enter them unto
the fire. It is an evil place indeed where they shall be entered."   (11:98)

About him and his army, Allāh ﷻ says in Sūrah Qasas,

وَأَتْبَعْنَاهُمْ فِيْ هٰذِهِ الدُّنْيَا لَعْنَةً وَّيَوْمَ الْقِيَامَةِ هُمْ مِّنَ الْمَقْبُوْحِيْنَ

"We set a curse after them in this world and on the Day of Judgement
they shall be among the hateful."   (28:42)

Allāh ﷻ concludes the Rukū by declaring, **"There is certainly a lesson in
this for the one who fears."** People who are concerned that they should
not suffer the same plight because of disobedience will heed the lessons
in the episode. However, those who are heedless of the warnings and
who do not care to apply their intelligence will continue to disobey Allāh
ﷻ.

Creation of the Heavens and the Earth

أَأَنتُمْ أَشَدُّ خَلْقًا أَمِ السَّمَآءُ بَنَاهَا . رَفَعَ سَمْكَهَا فَسَوَّاهَا . وَأَغْطَشَ لَيْلَهَا وَأَخْرَجَ
ضُحَاهَا . وَالْأَرْضَ بَعْدَ ذَلِكَ دَحَاهَا . أَخْرَجَ مِنْهَا مَآءَهَا وَمَرْعَاهَا . وَالْجِبَالَ أَرْسَاهَا .
مَتَاعًا لَّكُمْ وَلِأَنْعَامِكُمْ

27) Are you (mankind) more difficult to create or the sky (which is larger)? (If Allāh could create something as immense and magnificent as the sky, resurrecting mankind on the Day of Judgement is extremely easy for Him.) Allāh has created it (the sky).
28) He elevated (lifted) its roof (made it a tower above the earth) then He perfected it (so that no cracks are found).
29) He made its night dark and its daylight manifest (by the rising and setting of the sun).
30) Thereafter (after creating all this in the sky), Allāh spread out the earth.
31) He extracted from the earth her water and fodder (plants).
32) And firmly stationed the mountains.
33) All this (was done) for your benefit (use) and for the benefit of your animals (so that you can all have food to eat and water to drink).

Allāh ﷻ addresses those who reject the coming of Judgement Day. Are you more difficult to create or the sky? Because the sky is a much larger creation and contains so many phenomena, any person will understand that its creation was more difficult than the creation of a man. If Allāh ﷻ has the power to create the sky, He certainly has the power to resurrect man on the Day of Judgement. Not only did Allāh ﷻ create the sky, Allāh ﷻ also elevated its roof, perfected it, made its night dark and its day manifest.

Allāh ﷺ says in Sūrah Mu'min,

لَخَلْقُ السَّمَاوَاتِ وَالْأَرْضِ أَكْبَرُ مِنْ خَلْقِ النَّاسِ وَلٰكِنَّ أَكْثَرَ النَّاسِ لَا يَعْلَمُوْنَ

"The creation of the heavens and the earth is greater (more complex) than the creation of mankind, but most people (the disbelievers) do not know. (While admitting that Allāh created the heavens and the earth, the disbelievers refuse resurrection, although resurrection is easier.)" (40:57)

In Sūrah Yāseen, He says,

أَوَلَيْسَ الَّذِيْ خَلَقَ السَّمَاوَاتِ وَالْأَرْضَ بِقَادِرٍ عَلٰى أَنْ يَّخْلُقَ مِثْلَهُمْ بَلٰى وَهُوَ الْخَلَّاقُ الْعَلِيْمُ . إِنَّمَا أَمْرُهُ إِذَا أَرَادَ شَيْئًا أَنْ يَّقُوْلَ لَهُ كُنْ فَيَكُوْنُ

"Does the One Who created the heavens and the earth not have the power to create others like them? Why not? (He can create millions more because) He is the Prolific Creator, the All Knowing. When He wills anything (intends to do anything), His only command is to say, 'Be!' and it comes into being." (36:81)

وَالْأَرْضَ بَعْدَ ذٰلِكَ دَحَاهَا

"Thereafter Allāh spread out the earth." (79:30)

According to the verses of Sūrah Hā-Meem Sajdah, the earth was created before the heaven, but it was only spread out after the creation of the heaven.

"Say, 'Do you people really disbelieve in and ascribe partners to the Being Who created the earth in two days? It is He Who is the Lord of the universe. And Allāh has placed mountains on the surface of the earth, blessed the earth and stipulated the earths provisions in four complete days, (this is sufficient as a reply) for those who question (you about the creation of the earth). Thereafter, Allāh turned (His attention) to the sky, which was smoke, and said to it, as well as to the earth, 'Come to Us (submit to Us) willingly or unwillingly.' Both replied, 'We shall come willingly.'

Within two days, Allāh ﷻ then made the skies into seven skies, and issued a suitable command (to the angels occupying each sky).

$$وَالْجِبَالَ أَرْسَاهَا$$

"And firmly stationed the mountains."

Allāh ﷻ settled the mountains, made them firm and established them in their places.

$$مَتَاعًا لَّكُمْ وَلِأَنْعَامِكُمْ$$

"All of these benefits are for mankind and his animals."

Allāh ﷻ has spread out the earth, caused its springs to gush forth, brought forth its hidden benefits, caused its rivers to flow and caused its vegetation, trees and fruits to grow. He also made its mountains firm so that it (the earth) would be calmly settled with its dwellers. All of this is a means of beneficial enjoyment for mankind, providing them with cattle which they eat and ride upon. He has granted them these beneficial things for the period that they need them in this worldly abode, until the end of time and the expiration of this life.

Tremendous Calamity

فَإِذَا جَآءَتِ الطَّآمَّةُ الْكُبْرَى . يَوْمَ يَتَذَكَّرُ الْإِنسَانُ مَا سَعَى . وَبُرِّزَتِ الْجَحِيمُ لِمَن
يَرَى . فَأَمَّا مَن طَغَى . وَآثَرَ الْحَيَاةَ الدُّنْيَا . فَإِنَّ الْجَحِيمَ هِيَ الْمَأْوَى

34) So when the tremendous calamity befalls.
35) That Day, man will recall what he did.
36) And Jahannam will be manifest for those who look on.
37) As for the one who transgresses,
38) And who prefers the life of this world,
39) Then Jahannam shall certainly be his abode.

فَإِذَا جَآءَتِ الطَّآمَّةُ الْكُبْرَى

"So when the tremendous calamity befalls."

The tremendous calamity refers to the Day of Judgement. It has been called this because it will overcome every matter. It will be frightful and horrifying, as Allāh ﷻ says,

بَلِ السَّاعَةُ مَوْعِدُهُمْ وَالسَّاعَةُ أَدْهَى وَأَمَرُّ

"The fact is that Qiyāmah is their appointment and Qiyāmah will be more grievous and more bitter." (54:46)

The Arabic word الطَّآمَّةُ (Tāmmah) translated as 'calamity' is derived from the word طَمَّ 'Tamma' which refers to something that rises above and overwhelms everything. Hasan Basri ﷺ states, **"The tremendous calamity"** refers to the second blowing of the trumpet. When Qiyāmah takes place, every person will realise whether his deeds are good enough to take him to Jannah or whether they are lacking. On that Day, there will be only two groups, as Allāh ﷻ says in Sūrah Shū'ra,

$$فَرِيْقٌ فِي الْجَنَّةِ وَفَرِيْقٌ فِي السَّعِيْرِ$$

"A group shall be in Jannah, while another shall be in the blaze." (42:07)

Allāh ﷻ refers to these two groups separately. Firstly, He speaks about those who are destined for Jahannam, Allāh ﷻ says, **"As for the one who transgresses and who prefers the life of this world, then Jahannam shall certainly be his abode."**

In Sūrah A'lā, Allāh ﷻ mentions the same point,

$$بَلْ تُؤْثِرُوْنَ الْحَيَاةَ الدُّنْيَا . وَالْآخِرَةُ خَيْرٌ وَّأَبْقَى$$

"However, they (most people) prefer the life of this world, whereas the Ākhirah (Hereafter) is much better and much more lasting." (87:16-17)

How clearly Allāh ﷻ puts forward the differences of this world and the Hereafter. **"What (pleasures and wealth) is with you (in this world) shall come to an end and what is with Allāh (the pleasures of the Ākhirah) will last forever." (16:96)**

People generally cling to Kufr and refuse to accept Islām because they fear losing their wealth or positions. This displays their preference for this world over the Hereafter. It is for the same reason that we also commit sins. Chasing after wealth, fame and position leads people to commit sins, to neglect their Fardh obligations and to involve themselves in everything that violates Allāh's ﷻ commands. Unfortunately, as Muslims, we have engrossed ourselves so deeply in the world that we cannot find a way out of it. We are never content with what we have and always crave for more. Our chasing of wealth and accumulating will not cease until death overcomes us. However, then it will be too late.

At this point, an incident comes to mind which I mentioned in my book, 'Pearls of Wisdom'. I would like to share this thought-provoking story which beautifully displays the importance of contentment with what one has. As one of our pious predecessors said, "The one who is content is the one who is truly rich, even though he may not possess a single thing in the world."

The Story Begins...

An American investment banker was at the dock of a small Mexican village, when a small boat with just one fisherman docked. Inside the boat were several large yellow fin tunas. The American banker complimented the Mexican fisherman on the quality of his fish and asked how long it took him to catch them. The Mexican replied, "Only a little while." The American then asked why he did not stay out longer and catch more fish. The Mexican said he had enough to support his family's immediate needs. The American then asked, "What do you do with rest of your time?" The Mexican fisherman said, "I sleep late, fish a little, play with my children, take a siesta with my wife and roam into the village café bar each evening, where I eat and drink and meet my friends. I have a full and busy life." The American scorned, "I am a honoured MBA and I could help you. You should spend more time fishing and with the proceeds, buy a bigger boat. With the proceeds from the bigger boat, you can buy several boats. Eventually, you can have a fleet of fishing boats. Instead of selling your catch to a middleman, you could sell directly to the processor, eventually, opening your own cannery (factory). You could control the product, processing and distribution. You would need to leave this small coastal fishing village and move to Mexico City, then LA (Los Angeles) and eventually to New York City where you will run your expanding enterprise."

The Mexican fisherman asked, "But how long will all this take?" to

64

which the American replied, "15-20 years."
"But what then?"

The American laughed and said, "That's the best part. When the time is right, you would announce an I.P.O and sell your company stock to the public and become rich. You would make millions."

"Millions?! And then what?" asked the fisherman.

The American said, "Then you would retire, move to a small fishing village where you could sleep late, fish a little, play with your kids, take a siesta with your wife and stroll to the village in the evening where you could eat and drink and meet your friends."

Subhān-Allāh! This is exactly what we are doing.

The Reality of this World

A man was walking in the jungle. Suddenly, a lion came towards him and the man ran as fast as he could to escape from it. He noticed a well in front of him and he jumped inside, hoping to escape from the lion. As he was falling inside the well, he grabbed onto the rope and saved himself. The man was so relieved but when he looked down, he saw a big snake at the bottom of the well. It had its jaws wide open, ready to swallow him up. The man then looked up and saw two mice nibbling at the rope. A black mouse and a white mouse were both chewing into the rope. The man's heart was pounding as he wondered how he could escape from this. Then he noticed a honeycomb in front of him that had delicious honey dripping from it. He stuck his finger into the honey and put it inside his mouth. It was delicious and for a moment, he forgot about the lion, the snake, and the two mice chewing at the rope!

This example is like our reality in this world. The lion is like the Angel of death who is always looming above us. The snake is like our grave which all humans will face. The rope is like our life. The black mouse and white mouse are like the day and night which are always nibbling at our life (the rope). The honey is like this Dunya (world). With its sweetness, it makes us forget the purpose of our life and the reality of death.

The Holy Prophet ﷺ says,

مَا قَلَّ وَكَفَى خَيْرٌ مِّمَّا كَثُرَ وَأَلْهَى

"What is little but sufficient is better than that which is abundant but causes heedlessness." (Ibn Hibbān)

Another Hadeeth teaches us the important lesson of life,

حُبُّ الدُّنْيَا رَأْسُ كُلِّ خَطِيئَةٍ

"The love of the world is the root of all sins." (Baihaqi)

Once a person indulges in the world, he can never come out of it. It becomes an addiction. The Holy Prophet ﷺ draws our attention regarding two greedy people but both greedy for two completely different things.

مَنْهُوْمَانِ لَا يَشْبَعَانِ: مَنْهُوْمٌ فِي الْعِلْمِ لَا يَشْبَعُ مِنْهُ، وَمَنْهُوْمٌ فِي الدُّنْيَا لَا يَشْبَعُ مِنْهَا

"Two greedy people are never satisfied; one who is greedy for knowledge can never get enough of it and one who is greedy for worldly possessions can never get enough of them." (Baihaqi)

This craving for wealth remains with every individual till his last breath. For some people, it overtakes their lives and eventually destroys them.

The Hadeeth of Bukhāri and Muslim states, "Son of Ādam ﷺ becomes old but two things in him remains young; greed for wealth and greed for more life." (Bukhāri, Muslim, Tirmizi)

Fear of Allāh ﷻ

وَأَمَّا مَنْ خَافَ مَقَامَ رَبِّهِ وَنَهَى النَّفْسَ عَنِ الْهَوٰى . فَإِنَّ الْجَنَّةَ هِيَ الْمَأْوٰى

40) As for the one who fears standing before his Lord and who restrains himself from carnal passions,
41) Then Jannah shall definitely be his abode.

On the other hand, when a person gives preference to the life of the Hereafter, he will be conscious about leading a life of piety and will stay away from sins.

The person who fears standing for reckoning before Allāh ﷻ will receive two gardens of Jannah, as Allāh ﷻ says in Sūrah Ar-Rahmān,

وَلِمَنْ خَافَ مَقَامَ رَبِّهِ جَنَّتَانِ

"The one who fears standing in the presence of his Lord shall have two gardens." (55:46)

Sayyidunā Jābir ﷺ narrates that the Holy Prophet ﷺ said, "I fear most for my Ummah that they follow the dictates of their Nafs and that they entertain lengthy hopes. The desires of the Nafs prevent one from the truth and lengthy hopes makes one forget about the Ākhirah. This world is travelling and leaving while the Ākhirah is travelling and approaching. Each has its sons; so if you can avoid being a son of this world, then do so. Today, you are in the place of deeds (the world) where there is no reckoning and tomorrow you will be in the Ākhirah where there are no deeds (only reckoning)." (Mishkāt)

Whenever a person wants to do good and abstain from evil, his carnal self presents an obstacle. Ones carnal self wants only pleasure and enjoyment and loves the world for this. It has no inclination for the Hereafter because its concern is only for the pleasure of this world. It will therefore prompt a person to commit sin and to lead a life of recklessness. Thus, when a person gains control over his carnal self (his Nafs), he will be able to abstain from sins and will content himself with what is Halāl instead of Harām. Such people will attain the high ranks of Jannah.

The Holy Prophet 🕮 says, "Hellfire is veiled with desires and Paradise is veiled with displeasures." (Bukhāri, Muslim)

Imām Nawawi 🕮 writes that Paradise cannot be gained except by undertaking hardships (like fulfilling the obligations of Allāh 🕮 and refraining from His prohibitions) and that Hellfire is earned by indulging in vain desires.

The Holy Prophet 🕮 states a parable of an intelligent person and a person who carries vain hopes. He says, "The intelligent one is who subdues his lower self and works for what comes after death, and the foolish one is he who puts his lower self in pursuance of its desires and has vain hopes about Allāh 🕮."(Tirmizi, Ibn Mājah)

The person who subdues his lower self is that person who renders himself in complete obedience to the commands of Allāh 🕮. In this parable, the one who carries vain hopes about Allāh 🕮 is the one who thinks, "My Lord is the Most Generous and Merciful," and forgets that Allāh 🕮 also said,

يَا أَيُّهَا الْإِنْسَانُ مَا غَرَّكَ بِرَبِّكَ الْكَرِيمِ

"O man! What has seduced you from your Lord, Most
Beneficent?" (82:06)

Also,

نَبِّئْ عِبَادِي أَنِّي أَنَا الْغَفُورُ الرَّحِيمُ وَأَنَّ عَذَابِي هُوَ الْعَذَابُ الْأَلِيمُ

"Tell My servants that I am indeed, the Most Forgiving, Most Merciful
and that My chastisement will be indeed, the most grievous
chastisement." (15:49)

The soul is like a horse which would take its own course when it is without reigns, however, when subjugated by them, it follows. In this regards, Allāma Busayri ﷺ provides a beautiful parable: "The self is like a
child who, if you leave it alone, would grow up in love of suckling, but if
you wean, it will be weaned."
"Then keep its desires in check and be (in a state) that it does not over-
power you. Verily, lust when it overpowers humiliates and destroys.
(Qaseeda Burda)

When a person suppresses and restrains his lower self by abundant
Dhikrullāh (Remembrance of Allāh ﷻ), constant Mujāhadah (spiritual
effort) and Riyādah (ascetic discipline), then the Nafs is so cleansed and
purified that the desires that tempt him to evil are totally eliminated.
This is the special stage of Wilāyah (Divine friendship) which in the spiritual terminology is called 'Fanā-Fillāh'. Allāh ﷻ says regarding such
people, addressing the Shaytān,

إِنَّ عِبَادِي لَيْسَ لَكَ عَلَيْهِمْ سُلْطَانٌ

"Indeed, My servants are such that you have no power over
them." (15:42)

69

The Holy Prophet ﷺ says, "None of you can be a perfect believer unless his desires follow my teachings."   (Mishkāt)

Hence, none of us will be a perfect believer until our desires are not in conformance with what the Holy Prophet ﷺ came with.

Once the Nafs becomes fully trained and disciplined, it will enjoy the true pleasures of this world and be prepared in anticipation for the Hereafter. When this type of soul is about to depart from this temporary abode, Allāh ﷺ will address it,

يَٰٓأَيَّتُهَا النَّفْسُ الْمُطْمَئِنَّةُ . ارْجِعِي إِلَىٰ رَبِّكِ رَاضِيَةً مَّرْضِيَّةً . فَادْخُلِي فِي عِبَادِي . وَادْخُلِي جَنَّتِي

"(As for the sincere and devoted believers, Allāh will say to each of them), 'O contented soul (that has attained peace)! Return happily (being pleased with yourself) to your Lord as He is (well) pleased with you. Enter among My (chosen) bondsmen and enter My Jannah.'"
(89:27-30)

يَسْأَلُونَكَ عَنِ السَّاعَةِ أَيَّانَ مُرْسَاهَا . فِيمَ أَنْتَ مِنْ ذِكْرَاهَا . إِلَىٰ رَبِّكَ مُنْتَهَاهَا . إِنَّمَا أَنْتَ مُنْذِرُ مَنْ يَّخْشَاهَا . كَأَنَّهُمْ يَوْمَ يَرَوْنَهَا لَمْ يَلْبَثُوا إِلَّا عَشِيَّةً أَوْ ضُحَاهَا

42) They ask you when Qiyāmah will take place.

43) What have you to tell about it?

44) To your Lord belongs (the knowledge of) its term.

45) The Day when they see it, it will seem as if they lived only an evening or morning.

Addressing the Holy Prophet ﷺ, Allāh ﷺ says, **"They ask you when the Day of Judgement will take place."** The disbelievers actually asked about Qiyāmah mockingly because they did not really want to know when it will occur. Allāh ﷻ says to the Holy Prophet ﷺ, **"What have you to tell about it?"** The Holy Prophet ﷺ could not inform them about it because he was not informed about its date.

Final Hour

Allāh ﷻ says in Sūrah A'rāf,

$$ يَسْأَلُونَكَ عَنِ السَّاعَةِ أَيَّانَ مُرْسَاهَا قُلْ إِنَّمَا عِلْمُهَا عِندَ رَبِّي لَا يُجَلِّيهَا لِوَقْتِهَا إِلَّا هُوَ ثَقُلَتْ فِي السَّمَاوَاتِ وَالْأَرْضِ لَا تَأْتِيكُمْ إِلَّا بَغْتَةً يَسْأَلُونَكَ كَأَنَّكَ حَفِيٌّ عَنْهَا قُلْ إِنَّمَا عِلْمُهَا عِندَ اللهِ وَلَٰكِنَّ أَكْثَرَ النَّاسِ لَا يَعْلَمُونَ $$

"They ask you regarding Qiyāmah, when will it occur? Say, 'Its knowledge is only with my Lord. Only He will manifest it on its time. It will be weighty on the heavens and the earth and will appear suddenly. They ask you as if you have perfect knowledge of it. Say, 'The knowledge of this is only with Allāh, but most people do not know.'" (7:187)

In the famous Hadeeth referred to as Hadeeth Jibreel, Jibreel (عليه السلام) asks the Holy Prophet ﷺ, "Now tell me about the final hour." The Holy Prophet ﷺ replied, "The one who has been questioned knows no more than the one who has questioned." (Bukhāri, Muslim)

Allāh ﷻ says, **"You are a warner only to him who fears it."** Those who have no concern for Qiyāmah will not heed a thousand warnings of Qiyāmah. However, a single warning suffices for the one who is concerned about his plight in the Ākhirah.

Allāh ﷻ concludes the Sūrah by saying, **"The Day when they see it, it will seem as if they lived only an evening or morning."**

People persistently ask about the date of Qiyāmah as if they are looking forward to it. All they intend doing is to mock the belief. However, when they see Qiyāmah taking place before their very eyes, they will regret their ways and their lives of tens or even hundreds of years will seem less than a day. The life which they thought would never end, will seem like only a dream.

The word 'Ashiyyah' in Arabic is the time between noon until the setting of the sun and the word 'Duhā' is the time between sunrise and midday. In Sūrah Mu'minoon, it states that Allāh ﷻ will ask the people, **"How long did you stay on earth by the count of years? They will say, '(Years are far too long to use as a measure. More appropriately, we will say that) We stayed only a day or part of a day, but (to be certain) ask those who count (the angels who were recording our lives)." He (Allāh) will say, '(Although not a day or part of a day, the fact is certain that) you stayed only for a little while. If only you had known (this while living in the world, then you would not have wasted your precious time).'"**

May Allāh ﷻ give us the Tawfeeq to value our precious time and may he give us the ability to prepare for the inevitable life of the Hereafter. Āmeen.

Alhamdulillāh, the commentary of Sūrah Naziyāt has been completed on Saturday the 14th of December 2014 corresponding to 11th of Safar 1435 at 9:35am.

Sūrah Abas

He frowned
Revealed in Makkah

بِسْمِ اللهِ الرَّحْمٰنِ الرَّحِيْمِ

In the name of Allāh, the Most Compassionate, the Most Merciful.

عَبَسَ وَتَوَلّٰى . أَنْ جَاءَهُ الْأَعْمٰى . وَمَا يُدْرِيْكَ لَعَلَّهُ يَزَّكّٰى . أَوْ يَذَّكَّرُ فَتَنْفَعَهُ الذِّكْرٰى . أَمَّا مَنِ اسْتَغْنٰى . فَأَنْتَ لَهُ تَصَدّٰى . وَمَا عَلَيْكَ أَلَّا يَزَّكّٰى . وَأَمَّا مَنْ جَاءَكَ يَسْعٰى . وَهُوَ يَخْشٰى . فَأَنْتَ عَنْهُ تَلَهّٰى

1) He (the Holy Prophet) frowned and turned away,

2) Because a blind man came to him (interrupting him).

3) (O Prophet) how do you know that perhaps he (the blind man) will be (spiritually) purified (by your guidance)?

4) Or he may take heed and the advice will prove beneficial (useful) to him?

5) As for him (the Quraysh leader) who was indifferent (do not care).

6) To him do you attend (instead of attending to the blind sincere Muslim).

7) When there would be no blame on you if he is not purified (because they were not Muslims in the first place).

8) As for him (the blind Muslim) who comes running to you,

9) In fear (of Allāh)

10) To him you show indifference (give little attention).

Reason of Revelation

Sayyidunā Abdullāh Ibn Umm Maktoom ⟨⟩, an eminent Companion of the Holy Prophet ⟨⟩ was a blind person. It once happened that the Holy Prophet ⟨⟩ was engaged in a dialogue with some leaders of Quraysh in the matters of Imān (belief), when Sayyidunā Abdullāh Ibn Umm Maktoom ⟨⟩ arrived. As he was blind, he did not realise that the Holy Prophet ⟨⟩ was occupied with the leaders and he kept insisting, "Teach me the knowledge that Allāh ⟨⟩ has bestowed you with."

Since his arrival and approach disturbed the dialogue and complying to and fulfilling his request would interrupt what was being said to the leaders of Quraysh, the Holy Prophet ⟨⟩ ignored him, thinking he could speak to him at any other time. On the other hand, the opportunity to address the Quraysh leaders was rare and if any of them accepted Islām it would influence many others to follow as the saying goes, "People adopt the Deen of their leaders and kings."

According to the authentic books of Tafseer, it states that the Holy Prophet ⟨⟩ was speaking to Utbah Ibn Rabee'ah, Abū Jahal, Ubayy Ibn Khalaf, Umayyah Ibn Khalaf and Abbās Ibn Abdul Muttalib (who had until then not embraced Islām).

The Holy Prophet's ⟨⟩ reaction became evident on his face when he frowned and turned away from Sayyidunā Abdullāh Ibn Umm Maktoom ⟨⟩ and continued his discourse with the Quraysh leaders. When the meeting broke up, the verses of Sūrah Abas were revealed to inform Allāh's ⟨⟩ dislike for this attitude and to give directions and advice for the future.

This attitude of the Holy Prophet ⟨⟩ was based on Ijtihād or an opinion based on personal reasoning. He thought that if a Muslim was to adopt a speech style that is not conforming with the etiquettes of a gathering, he

74

needs to be reprimanded, so that in the future he may be careful. That is the reason why he turned his face away from Sayyidunā Abdullāh Ibn Umm Maktoom ﷺ. Secondly, disbelief (Kufr) and polytheism (Shirk) are the most severe of sins and an effort to eradicate them should take priority over the subsidiary precepts of Islām which Sayyidunā Abdullāh Ibn Umm Maktoom ﷺ was seeking.

Through this Sūrah, Allāh ﷻ confirmed the incorrectness of Ijtihād of the Holy Prophet ﷺ and explained to him that educating a genuine seeker will most certainly benefit him, while the benefit of discussion with the opponents (who disrespectfully turn their faces away when the Holy Prophet ﷺ talks to them) is shaky and doubtful. A doubtful thing cannot be preferred over certainty.

As for the violation of etiquette committed by Sayyidunā Abdullāh Ibn Umm Maktoom ﷺ, its excuse is pointed out by the Holy Qur'ān in the word 'blind.' It is indicated by this word that being a blind man, he could not see what the Holy Prophet ﷺ was doing and with whom he was engaged in conversation. Thus, he was excusable and was not liable to be subjected to aversion. This indicates that if an excusable person were to break any rule of etiquette unwillingly, he should not be reprimanded.

"He frowned and turned away." (80:1)

The reference here is to the Holy Prophet ﷺ who is being addressed, thus the verb should have been in the second person i.e. you frowned and you turned away. However, the Holy Qur'ān, on this occasion uses the third person in order to maintain the honour of the Holy Prophet ﷺ as if this attitude was shown by some other person. In a subtle way, it alludes to the point that what the Holy Prophet ﷺ did was not befitting of his high status. Then the next sentence,

$$وَمَا يُدْرِيكَ لَعَلَّهُ يَزَّكَّى$$

"And how do you know that perhaps he will be purified," (80:3)

alludes to the fact that the Holy Prophet 🌸 was excusable, because it did not come to his attention that Sayyidunā Abdullāh Ibn Umm Maktoom ؏ was asking for something which had a certain positive effect whereas the effect of the conversation on the others was doubtful and dubious.

The second sentence abandons the third person and switches to the second person in order to maintain the honour of the Holy Prophet 🌸. Had he not been addressed in second person at all, it might have created the impression that he was not being addressed directly by Allāh ﷻ because of his unapproved conduct, which would have been an unbearable pain and grief for the Holy Prophet 🌸. Just as the third person in the first statement is meant to show respect to him, the second person in the following sentence is also meant to honour and console him.

On this particular juncture, the Holy Qur'ān uses the word يَزَّكَّى 'Yazzakkā' (He will be purified). This statement suggests that 'he will be purified' whilst in the next verse, it states, **"He may take heed and the advice will prove beneficial to him?"** The first statement refers to the righteous and pious person who cleanses his internal and external self. The second statement is that of a Mubtadi (beginner) on the spiritual journey. At this stage, the beginner is reminded of Allāh ﷻ which enhances the greatness and awe of Allāh ﷻ in his heart. The two sentences are joined by the particle 'or' and technically, they are not necessarily exclusive to one another. The point is that Sayyidunā Abdullāh Ibn Umm Maktoom ؏ would have attained either both the benefits or at least the second one, that is, increase in Allāh's ﷻ remembrance and in His awe which is the initial step towards perfection.   (Mazhari)

Qur'anic Principle

On this specific juncture, the Holy Prophet ﷺ was faced with two different requirements at the same time. On the one hand, he was required to
teach a Muslim and to encourage him in attaining perfection. On the other hand, he had to provide guidance to non-Muslims. The principle laid
down here makes it clear that the first requirement takes priority over
the second one. It is improper to delay the first task (educating Muslims)
because of the second task. This indicates that education of Muslims and
their reform is more important and takes priority over getting the non-
Muslims to embrace the faith. Scholars should avoid any such indul-
gence and engrossment when disposing of any doubts of the non-
Muslims, which may create doubts or complaints in the minds of the
general Muslims. Scholars, preachers, reformers and teachers need to
keep in mind these Qur'anic guidelines to maintain the welfare and priority of the Muslims.

True Believers

The forthcoming verses clarify the above principle more elaborately, **"As
for the one who was indifferent, to him do you attend."**
In other words, those who turn away from you and your religion, you
are pursuing, under the hope that somehow they should become Muslims, while this is not your responsibility. If they do not embrace the
faith, there will be no blame on you.

Allāh ﷻ continues, **"As for him who comes running to you in fear, to him
you show indifference."** Imām Qurtubi ﷺ writes that although the Holy
Prophet's ﷺ intention was laudable, Allāh ﷻ reprimanded him because
the hearts of the men of Suffa should not be hurt and to make it clear
that a poor Mu'min (believer) is better than a wealthy disbeliever. The
message here is the same as contained in Sūrah An'ām, verse 52, where
Allāh ﷻ says,

77

وَلَا تَطْرُدِ الَّذِينَ يَدْعُوْنَ رَبَّهُمْ بِالْغَدَاةِ وَالْعَشِيّ يُرِيْدُوْنَ وَجْهَهُ مَا عَلَيْكَ مِنْ حِسَابِهِمْ مِّنْ شَيْءٍ وَّمَا مِنْ حِسَابِكَ عَلَيْهِمْ مِّنْ شَيْءٍ فَتَطْرُدَهُمْ فَتَكُوْنَ مِنَ الظَّالِمِيْنَ

"Do not shun those who call unto their Lord morning and evening, aspiring for His pleasure. You are not accountable at all for them, nor are they at all accountable for you, that you shun them and become of the oppressors."   (6:52)

The same message is also conveyed in Sūrah Kahf, where Allāh ﷻ says,

وَاصْبِرْ نَفْسَكَ مَعَ الَّذِيْنَ يَدْعُوْنَ رَبَّهُمْ بِالْغَدَاةِ وَالْعَشِيّ يُرِيْدُوْنَ وَجْهَهُ وَلَا تَعْدُ عَيْنَاكَ عَنْهُمْ تُرِيْدُ زِيْنَةَ الْحَيَاةِ الدُّنْيَا

"Restrain yourself with those who, seeking His pleasure, call to their Lord morning and evening and do not shift your attention from them with the intent of acquiring the adornment of this worldly life."   (18:28)

After the revelation of this Sūrah, the Holy Prophet ﷺ showed special regard for Sayyidunā Abdullāh Ibn Umm Maktoom ؓ. When the Holy Prophet ﷺ used to see him approach, he would say, "Welcome to the one concerning whom my Lord has reprimanded me." The Holy Prophet ﷺ would then spread his Chādar (cloak) for him to sit and would ask him several times if he needed anything. Furthermore, as an atonement, it is stated in the different books of Tafseer and Hadeeth that the Holy Prophet ﷺ appointed Sayyidunā Abdullāh Ibn Umm Maktoom ؓ as governor of Madeenah thirteen times when he left on expeditions. In the Holy Prophet's ﷺ absence, Sayyidunā Abdullāh Ibn Umm Maktoom ؓ was in charge of affairs in Madeenah and he would lead the Salāh.

Holy Scriptures

كَلَّا إِنَّهَا تَذْكِرَةٌ ۚ فَمَن شَاءَ ذَكَرَهُ ۚ فِى صُحُفٍ مُّكَرَّمَةٍ ۚ مَّرْفُوعَةٍ مُّطَهَّرَةٍ ۚ بِأَيْدِي
سَفَرَةٍ ۚ كِرَامٍ بَرَرَةٍ

11) This should never be. Indeed, this (Qur'ān) is a reminder (so that mistakes are not repeated).

12) So whoever desires should remember it (the advice of the Qur'ān).

13) (It, the Qur'ān is recorded) in scriptures (the Lawhul-Mahfooz) that are honoured (in the sight of Allāh).

14) Elevated (just beneath Allāh's throne) and pure (from errors and beyond the reach of the impure Shayāteen).

15) In the hands of scribes (the angels and the Sahābah who were the scribes).

16) Who are honourable and righteous.

In these verses, Allāh ﷻ reprimands us through the Holy Prophet ﷺ that this situation should never occur i.e. one should never ignore a believer who comes to him to learn Deen because the Holy Qur'ān is a reminder, "So whoever desires should remember it."

The duty of the Holy Prophet ﷺ was to propagate the message of Islām and he was not responsible to make people believe. Likewise, as Muslims, our duty is to convey the message of Deen and we are not compelled to get people to embrace Islām. If anyone refused to believe, it was to his own detriment and loss and his disbelief would not harm the Holy Prophet ﷺ in the least.

Allāh ﷻ describes the Holy Qur'ān itself when He says, "(It is) in scriptures that are honoured, elevated and pure (in Allāh's sight because the Shayāteen cannot reach there), in the hands of scribes who are honour-

able and righteous." The Holy Qur'ān is preserved in the Lawhul-Mahfooz (Preserved Tablet) where noble and pious angels record events. Imām Ahmad ﷺ recorded from Sayyidah Āishah ﷺ that the Holy Prophet ﷺ said, "He who recites the Holy Qur'ān proficiently, will be with the noble, righteous, ambassador angels and the one who recites it with difficulty will receive two rewards." (Ahmad, Muslim)

The word 'Suhuf' refers to Lawhul-Mahfooz. Although it is a single thing, but 'Suhuf', the plural form of 'Saheefah' is used because all Divine Scriptures are written in it or because the angels copy their scriptures from them. The word مَرْفُوعَةٍ 'Marfoo'ah' means exalted in the sight of Allāh ﷺ. The word مُطَهَّرَةٍ 'Mutahharah' (purified) refers to the fact that people in the state of major impurities (i.e. Janābah, menstrual discharge, post-natal bleeding and also those in the state of minor impurities) are not permitted to touch it.

"In the hands of scribes." The word سَفَرَةٍ 'Safarah', with fathah on the first two letters, may be the plural of 'Sāfir' which means scribe. In this case, it would refer to the recording angels or to the Prophets and those Companions who wrote down the revelation.

The word 'Safarah' may also be used as the plural of 'Safeer' in the meaning of envoy or ambassador. In this case, it would refer to the angels who convey the revelation. The scholars of this Ummah are also included in this term, because they too are envoys between the Holy Prophet ﷺ and the Ummah.

In another verse, Allāh ﷺ describes the attributes of the Arch Angel, Jibreel ﷺ, who is an envoy between Allāh ﷺ and the Holy Prophet ﷺ.

إِنَّهُ لَقَوْلُ رَسُولٍ كَرِيمٍ . ذِي قُوَّةٍ عِنْدَ ذِي الْعَرْشِ مَكِينٍ . مُّطَاعٍ ثَمَّ أَمِينٍ

"Undoubtedly this Qur'ān is a word brought (from Allāh to the Holy Prophet) by an honourable (noble) messenger (Jibreel), who is powerful and of high rank (status) in the sight of the Owner of the Throne. He is also obeyed (by the angels in the heavens) and is trustworthy (and will therefore, never corrupt any message Allāh sends with him)." (18:19-21)

In contrast to this, Allāh ﷻ refuses any involvement of evil in connection to the Holy Qur'ān. He eloquently says, **"The Shayāteen have not brought it (the Qur'ān) down. It (bringing down the Qur'ān) is not suited to them (because while the Holy Qur'ān provides guidance, the Shayāteen only provide misguidance) nor have they the capability (to over hear any part of the Holy Qur'ān in the heavens before it was transmitted to the Holy Prophet because Allāh had sealed off the corridors to the heavens for them and whoever tried to overhear something was destroyed by a flaming star). They (the Shayāteen) have definitely been forbidden from listening (to the revelation of the Qur'ān in the heavens)."** (26:210:212)

Ingratitude of Man

قُتِلَ الْإِنْسَانُ مَا أَكْفَرَهُ . مِنْ أَيِّ شَيْءٍ خَلَقَهُ . مِنْ نُطْفَةٍ خَلَقَهُ فَقَدَّرَهُ . ثُمَّ السَّبِيلَ
يَسَّرَهُ . ثُمَّ أَمَاتَهُ فَأَقْبَرَهُ . ثُمَّ إِذَا شَاءَ أَنْشَرَهُ . كَلَّا لَمَّا يَقْضِ مَا أَمَرَهُ .

17) Woe be to man (the disbeliever)! How ungrateful is he (despite all the favours Allāh has blessed him with, the disbeliever chooses to worship others instead)!

18) From what did Allāh create him?

19) From a drop of semen, Allāh created him, then made him in due

81

proportion (with all the parts of his body in proportion to each other).
20) Then He eased the way for him (to come into this world and to survive in it by sending the Prophets and the Divine Scriptures. Allāh also made it easy for man to understand right and wrong).
21) Then Allāh gave him death and concealed him in a grave.
22) Then Allāh shall resurrect him when He wills.
23) Behold! Man has not done what Allāh has commanded him.

These verses discuss man's ingratitude and his creation. Allāh ﷻ says, **"Woe be to man! How ungrateful is he?."** Allāh ﷻ created man and showered innumerable favours on him but he does not thank Allāh ﷻ for them. Even worse is that man refuses to accept Allāh ﷻ as his Rabb (Lord).

How beautifully Allāh ﷻ reminds us of His favours. He states, **"He grants you whatever you ask of Him. If you try (repeatedly) to count Allāh's bounties, you will never be able to do so. Indeed, man is extremely unjust and very ungrateful (because he fails to obey Allāh despite all that Allāh does for him)." (14:34)**

Reality of Man

If man ponders over his beginning, he will truly humble himself before Allāh ﷻ. Allāh ﷻ developed the sperm cell from its original lowly state and eventually fashioned a human being with functioning organs and limbs. Time and time again, Allāh ﷻ reminds us about our beginning and our origin so we express our gratitude to Him for all His blessings.
Once, Yazeed Ibn Muhallab was walking on the streets with haughtiness and pride. Mutarrif ﷺ, a pious elder, saw him in that state and advised him, "O my son! Allāh ﷻ dislikes this type of attitude and the manner of walking."

Yazeed Ibn Muhallāb retorted, "Don't you know who I am?" A typical reply of our youngsters nowadays which they resort to when they are questioned or if one objects to their misbehaviour.

Mutarrif ﷺ replied, "I verily know who you are;

اَوَّلُكَ نُطْفَةٌ قَذِرَةٌ وَّاٰخِرُكَ جِيْفَةٌ مَّنِذِرَةٌ وَّاَنْتَ بَيْنَ ذٰلِكَ حَامِلُ عَذِرَةٍ

Your origin is an impure semen and your end will be a decomposed body and in the interim you are carrying waste in your body."

Subhān-Allāh! This is the condition of every one of us. Let us ponder over these profound words of this pious person and reflect on them on a daily basis. Constant Murāqabah (meditation) on these words will eventually erase and eradicate the malady of pride and arrogance which is a deadly spiritual disease. Allāh ﷺ addresses mankind, **"O man! What has cast you into deception concerning your Most Generous Rabb? (Why do you continue sinning believing that Allāh will always forgive you because He is generous?"** This attitude shows disloyalty to Allāh Who has blessed man with innumerable bounties).

الَّذِيْ خَلَقَكَ فَسَوَّاكَ فَعَدَلَكَ . فِيْ اَيِّ صُوْرَةٍ مَّا شَاۤءَ رَكَّبَكَ

"The One Who has created you, perfected (shaped) you, gave you (your body) due proportion and made you in the fashion He desired (without making you into something despicable)." (82:6-8)

Allāh ﷺ says in Sūrah Qiyāmah,

اَلَمْ يَكُ نُطْفَةً مِّنْ مَّنِيٍّ يُّمْنٰى . ثُمَّ كَانَ عَلَقَةً فَخَلَقَ فَسَوّٰى

"Was he (man) not a discharge of semen (in the womb at one stage)? After which, he developed into a clot of blood and then, He (Allāh) created him and perfected him?" (75:37-38)

83

After creating man, Allāh ﷻ then eased the way for him. Allāh ﷻ led the foetus through the various stages of its development and when the child was ready to be born, Allāh ﷻ made it possible for it to emerge through an extremely narrow exit (the vaginal passage).

Mufti Shafee Sāhib ﷫ writes, 'Allāh ﷻ, through His infinite wisdom, creates man in his mother's womb, stage after stage, within three layers of darkness (i.e the stomach, the womb and the membrane - in which the foetus develops). It is kept in a safe place in the stomach. The mother, in whose stomach all this is happening, is totally unaware of the details of this process. Thereafter, when the baby becomes perfect, with all its limbs and organs, Allāh ﷻ made it possible that a body, weighing 3 to 4kg, comes out through an extremely narrow passage and the mother does not suffer unduly. So blessed be He Who is the Best Creator!'

When a child is in the mother's womb, his head is upright towards his mother's head and his legs are downwards towards his mother's feet. However, Subhān-Allāh, when the time of birth draws near, Allāh ﷻ inspires the child and immediately, it turns its direction and its feet go upwards and its head goes downwards, in order to facilitate the easy delivery. Once the child comes to the outside world, Allāh ﷻ has made his sustenance easy for him, to such an extent, that it is very close to him and he just has to cling to his mother's breast and commence his drinking. He continues to achieve this blessing by his crying which implies to his need for food. Allāh ﷻ continues to bless him with various nourishments and bounties till he grows up to be a mature person. When he reaches this stage, he is guided by his intellect to choose the right path which has been indicated by the numerous Prophets and Messengers sent by Allāh ﷻ for the guidance of mankind. Hence, in every aspect, Allāh ﷻ has made his matters easy for him.

Furthermore, Allāh ﷻ then gives him death and concealed him in a grave. Life and death are in Allāh's ﷻ control. Man has no control over life, no control over death and no control over the life after death. Allāh ﷻ has taught man to bury the dead because the burial is most befitting for man's honour. Leaving a corpse above the ground to be ravaged by animals that scatter the bones about does not accord man's body the respect it deserves. Everybody, therefore, gets the respect it deserves. The treatment it receives after the burial depends on the deeds of the person in this world.

There are certain nations who cremate their dead and others who feed their dead to creatures. These are nations who do not follow a Divine religion and therefore, are grossly misguided. However, even their dead eventually end up in the ground because the ashes of the deceased come to rest on the ground and the vultures that devoured the corpse become dust after their death. In this regard, Allāh ﷻ says in Sūrah Mursalāt,

$$ أَلَمۡ نَجۡعَلِ الۡأَرۡضَ كِفَاتًا . أَحۡيَآءً وَّأَمۡوَاتًا $$

"Have We not made the earth consist of both the living and the dead?" (77:25-26)

After mentioning the inception of human life, in this verse, Allāh ﷻ points to its end which is death and the grave. Death has been mentioned here in the context of a blessing rather than a calamity. The Holy Prophet ﷺ is reported to have mentioned it in such a light, "The gift of a believer is death." Moreover, there is a profound wisdom in death at macro-level for the entire world. If there was no death and people continued to live eternally, there would be utter chaos on the surface of earth. Subhān-Allāh!

Furthermore, by giving death, a person can achieve his result and award for the effort and struggle he carried out in this world. If there was no death, he could have been continuously striving without any results or breaks. Our pious predecessors have stated, "Death is a bridge which connects a beloved with his beloved."

Allāh ﷻ has said, ثُمَّ أَمَاتَهُ فَأَقْبَرَهُ. The Arabic word, 'Iqbār' has been used which means to order for the burial. This indicates towards the fact that it is obligatory to bury a dead human body after it is given a proper Ghusl and enshrouded in clean clothes (Kafn). On the other hand, the word 'Qabara' means to bury. In Arabic, it is used to mean to bury the dead.

The first incident of burial in the history of mankind occurred when Qābeel (one of the sons of Ādam عليه السلام) killed his brother Hābeel. This was the first ever death on the surface of earth. Hence, Qābeel did not have any idea what to do with the corpse. He enshrouded the dead body with a Chādar (cloth) and contemplated what he should do with his dead brother's corpse. He eventually reached a jungle and sat down in a state of grief. Whilst seated in this state of utter confusion and distress, he observed two crows in front of him. The two crows suddenly started to fight amongst themselves. Ultimately, one killed the other. Then, the surviving crow started to dig, remove the sand and bury the dead crow into the grave. This incident directed Qābeel to bury his brother in a similar manner.

Allāh ﷻ mentions the story of Hābeel and Qābeel in Sūrah Mā'idah and concludes with the incident of the burial of Hābeel. Allāh ﷻ says,

فَبَعَثَ اللهُ غُرَابًا يَّبْحَثُ فِي الْأَرْضِ لِيُرِيَهُ كَيْفَ يُوَارِيْ سَوْءَةَ أَخِيْهِ قَالَ يَا وَيْلَتَا

أَعَجَزْتُ أَنْ أَكُونَ مِثْلَ هٰذَا الْغُرَابِ فَأُوَارِيَ سَوْءَةَ أَخِي فَأَصْبَحَ مِنَ النَّادِمِينَ

"(After killing his brother, Qābeel did not know what to do with the corpse because no human had died previously). Then, Allāh sent a crow to dig (a hole in) the earth to show him how to conceal the corpse of his brother. (Seeing the crow dig a hole to bury a dead crow in it), he (Qābeel) cried out, 'Woe unto me that I could not be like this crow and conceal the body of my brother!' So he became one of the remorseful ones (because he did know something that a crow knew and because he did not know how to face his father." (5:31)

Then when Sayyidunā Ādam عليه السلام passed away, the angels descended and practically showed the Ghusl, Kafn and Dafn. Hence, this became the practice from then till the present day. As mentioned earlier, the Islamic rituals in respect to Ghusl (bathing) Kafn (shrouding) and Dafn (burial) all demonstrate the respect and dignity offered to the body even after its death.

Those who cremate or burn the body object to the burial by saying that it creates bad and offensive odour, whilst cremating eradicates the foul smell. One reply to this is that fire is a destroyer. Anything allocated to the fire is destroyed and consumed by it whereas, the earth is trustworthy. Anything you allocate to the earth is preserved by it. Therefore, it is better to assign and allocate our dead to the earth than allocate it to the fire. It is the nature of man and even animals, that if they want to preserve and safeguard anything, e.g. treasure and wealth, they preserve it in the earth and if they want to destroy anything, they burn it.

Secondly, as Muslims we believe that the souls will return back to the body, hence, we wait for that by burying our dead. Burning and cremating the body is contrary to this belief.

It is also worth noting that it is of the highest disrespect to burn the supreme creation of Allāh ﷻ with your own hands and throw the ashes into the air. This type of behaviour is only done with impure and degraded substances and matters. When we intend to preserve and safeguard anything precious, then the best solution is to hide and conceal it under the ground.

For those who say that fire erases the bad odour whilst earth, on the contrary decomposes and creates offensive odour. The reply is that this objection would only be accepted if we intend to take out the body again. In the case of burial, there is no intention of re-digging the grave and taking out the corpse. Hence, the odour will have no effect on the humans living on the ground.

Also, the general principle is, 'Everything should return to its original state.' Hence, man is created from earth so it should be returned to it, as it is clearly mentioned in the Holy Qur'ān, **"We have created you (your father Ādam) from it (the earth), shall return you to it (when you are buried), and will extract (restore) you from it a second time (when you will all come out from your graves on the Day of Judgement)." (20:55)**

Burning the corpse is against this natural principle of life because fire is the primary substance used for the creation of Jinn and Shayāteen and not human beings. Hence, burying the human being is in actual fact, returning it back to its original state.

An incident is narrated regarding a Muslim army which entered a non-Muslim country. In that particular area where the Muslim army halted, there was an intelligent Hindu who addressed the Muslim army, "I have found out about Islām and accept all the commandments and rituals to be good, wholesome and according to nature. However, one thing I find unacceptable is that you bury your dead and do not burn them. Burying creates bad odours whilst burning eradicates that."

An individual from the Muslim army who was a Faqeeh (jurist) replied, Before I answer your question, please reply to my question then I will reply to your objection." The Hindu said, "Ask?"

The scholar said, "Imagine, a person settles in a particular country, marries a woman and also hires a woman as a cook. He has a child from his wife and then a need arises for him to embark on a journey. Who will he allocate the child to, the cook or the mother of the child?"

The Hindu replied, "In the presence of the mother, the child will never be handed to the cook, because the child is the mother's not the cook's."

The scholar said, "Yes, correct. In the same way, when the Rooh (soul) came from the heavens to the earth, it came into the appearance and form of earth. All its benefits - food, clothing, residence etc were achieved via the earth. The fire only cooks something which is raw. Hence, the mother of the person is the earth and the cook is the fire. When it (the Rooh) wants to leave for Ālam Barzakh, it leaves its body to its mother - the earth, not the cook - the fire. The Hindu was astounded and accepted Islām.

Another argument of burying the dead is that in keeping the body intact, it stays in one particular place paving the way for the family, relatives and friends to visit the graveyard and continue sending Sadaqah Jāriyah in the form of Tilāwat (recitation) of the Holy Qur'ān, Tasbeeh and Durood Shareef. By burning it, its identity and place of existence will be destroyed.

$$\text{ثُمَّ إِذَا شَاءَ أَنْشَرَهُ}$$

"Then Allāh shall resurrect him when He wills."

Allāh ﷻ states further that after creating man, perfecting him and causing him to die, death is not the end of a person. After death, people have
to account for whatever they did in this world and face the rewards or
punishment they deserve.

**"No! Man has certainly not expressed gratitude. (In addition to this,)
man has not done what Allāh has commanded him."**
Some commentators state that this refers to breaching the pledge in
which man pledged to acknowledge only Allāh ﷻ as his Rabb (Lord).
Then he breached the pledge after coming to this world. The verse could
also refer to man's disobeying of the commands of the Prophets and
Messengers, and what is contained in the Divine Scriptures. Of course,
the verse refers to the condition of man in general and to all of mankind
collectively.

<u>**Contemplation on the Blessings of Allāh ﷻ**</u>

$$\text{فَلْيَنْظُرِ الْإِنْسَانُ إِلَى طَعَامِهِ . أَنَّا صَبَبْنَا الْمَاءَ صَبًّا . ثُمَّ شَقَقْنَا الْأَرْضَ شَقًّا . فَأَنْبَتْنَا}$$
$$\text{فِيهَا حَبًّا . وَعِنَبًا وَقَضْبًا . وَزَيْتُونًا وَنَخْلًا . وَحَدَائِقَ غُلْبًا . وَفَاكِهَةً وَأَبًّا . مَتَاعًا لَّكُمْ}$$
$$\text{وَلِأَنْعَامِكُمْ}$$

24) Let man look at his food.
25) We make the rain pour forth in abundance.
26) Then we cause the earth to part into clefts.
27) We then grow on the earth grains,
28) grapes, vegetables,

29) olives, date palms,
30) dense gardens,
31) fruits and fodder,
32) for your benefit and for the benefit of your animals.

Allāh ﷻ commands man to reflect for a while. Allāh ﷻ says, **"Let man look at his food."** Man should ponder about the various types of food that Allāh ﷻ causes to grow from the ground, such as grains, grapes, vegetables, olives, date palms, dense gardens, fruit and fodder. Allāh ﷻ has created fruit for enjoyment and fodder for man's animals. Then too, these fruits and other food do not grow sparsely so that only one or two are available. Allāh ﷻ causes them to grow in abundance from huge plantations so that entire nations are fed.

Have we ever pondered, when we sit down to eat our daily meal, over the different varieties of food that are present in front of us? These different types of food have in many cases, travelled thousands of miles through the effort and labour of thousands of human beings and animals before being placed on our plates. This is the sheer grace of Allāh ﷻ, hence we praise Him by supplicating, **"All praises to Allāh, Who fed us and gave us drink and made us Muslims."**

Allāh ﷻ has made the rain a means for all these foods to grow. When the rain seeps into the ground, Allāh ﷻ causes the seed of the plant to split and the shoot to sprout from it. Referring to this, Allāh says, **"We make the rain pour forth in abundance. Then We cause the earth to part into clefts."** Allāh ﷻ has taken care of all this, **"For your benefit and for the benefit of your animals."** Man should ponder about these phenomena and express gratitude to Allāh ﷻ for all of this.

Horrors of Judgement Day

فَإِذَا جَاءَتِ الصَّاخَّةُ . يَوْمَ يَفِرُّ الْمَرْءُ مِنْ أَخِيهِ . وَأُمِّهِ وَأَبِيهِ . وَصَاحِبَتِهِ وَبَنِيهِ . لِكُلِّ امْرِئٍ مِّنْهُمْ يَوْمَئِذٍ شَأْنٌ يُغْنِيهِ . وُجُوهٌ يَّوْمَئِذٍ مُّسْفِرَةٌ . ضَاحِكَةٌ مُّسْتَبْشِرَةٌ . وَوُجُوهٌ يَّوْمَئِذٍ عَلَيْهَا غَبَرَةٌ . تَرْهَقُهَا قَتَرَةٌ . أُولَئِكَ هُمُ الْكَفَرَةُ الْفَجَرَةُ

33) So when the deafening scream will come.
34) On that Day, man will flee from his brother,
35) his mother, his father.
36) his wife and his sons.
37) On that Day, every one of them will be preoccupied with a predicament that will make him oblivious of another.
38) On that Day, many faces shall be radiant.
39) Laughing and happy.
40) And on that day, many faces will be dusty.
41) Covered in darkness.
42) Those will be the sinful disbelievers.

Allāh ﷻ paints the picture of the Day of Judgement in these verses. Allāh ﷻ says, **"So when the deafening scream will come (i.e. the second blowing of the trumpet), on that Day man will flee from his brother, his mother, his father, his wife and his sons. On that day every one of them will be preoccupied with a predicament that will make him oblivious of another."**

Sayyidunā Abdullāh Ibn Abbās ؓ said, "'As-Sākhah' is one of the names of the Day of Judgement that Allāh ﷻ has magnified and warned his servants of." Ibn Jareer At-Tabari ؒ said, "It is a name for the blowing into the trumpet." Imām Al Baghawi ؒ said, "'As-Sākhah' means the

92

thunderous shout of the Day of Judgement.

It has been called this because it will deafen the ears. This means that it pierces the hearing to such an extent, that it almost deafens the ears.

The scholars of Tafseer have mentioned why a person will run away from all these close relatives, even though in the world, he was willing to sacrifice his life for them. The reasons are:
1) Due to the fear that if they see him, they will demand their rights which he did not fulfil e.g. like a debtor runs from the creditor. Hence, on the Day of Judgement, a person will flee from his acquaintances more than the strangers lest they demand their rights.
2) Fearing that they will beg for intercession or assistance which he will be unable to fulfil. He will be overwhelmed with worries, fearing that his relatives who have been destined for Hell will ask for intercession and he will be obliged to free them from it, by giving away either his good deeds, or by him taking some of their sins. Hence, we see in this world, a person turns away from his relatives at the time of famine or drought, lest they ask for any assistance. So what will be the condition on that horrifying day?
3) He will flee from them due to the fact that he will have to confront the pain of bearing them being punished whilst he will not be able to avert the torment or have the power to intercede.

The reality is, people will flee for all these reasons, some will flee for one of the above reasons, some for two and some for all three reasons.

Allāh ﷻ commences the verse with the brother i.e. that he will flee from his brother, giving him priority over other people in the world. This is because despite the natural attachment he had with him, having that close relationship from childhood, he will still flee from him on that day.

Allāh ﷻ then mentions the mother because a person has more love and affection for the mother than a brother. This is followed by the father, because even though a person has more responsibility and duty in terms of Khidmat (service) to a mother, in terms of respect and honour, the father has more priority.

After the parents, Allāh ﷻ mentions the spouse. A person has a deeper connection with his spouse than anyone else, even more so than the parents because as husband and wife, they stayed together until death separated them. Many a times, a person prioritises his wife over his parents. However, on that terrifying day, he will even run away from her.

Lastly, Allāh ﷻ mentions the sons because man has most affection and love for them due to the fact that they will continue to keep his name alive after his death and they will take his place and continue on with his noble causes.

In Tafseer Azeezi, Shah Abdul Aziz ﷺ mentions that the first person who will run away from his brother on that Day will be Qābeel from his brother Hābeel, fearing that he will demand his blood money from him. The first person to run away from his parents will be Sayyidunā Ibraheem عليه السلام, fearing that his parents will request for intercession, which will not be acceptable on their behalf due to them being disbelievers. The first individual to run away from his spouse will be Sayyidunā Loot عليه السلام. He will run away from his wife who according to the text of the Holy Qur'ān, was a disbeliever and a hypocrite. Thus, no intercession will be accepted on her behalf due to her disbelief and hypocrisy. The first person to run away from his son will be Sayyidunā Nooh عليه السلام who will run away from his son, Kan'ān who died as a disbeliever.

In the Hadeeth of Bukhāri and Muslim, it is stated that mankind will plead to all the mighty Messengers to intercede on their behalf on that

94

day but each of them will say, "O' myself! O' myself! Today, I will not ask you (O' Allāh 🕮) concerning anyone but myself." Even Eesa Ibn Maryam ﷺ will say, "I will not ask Him (Allāh 🕮) concerning anyone but myself today. I will not even ask regarding Maryam, the woman who gave birth to me." Thus Allāh 🕮 says,

$$\text{يَوْمَ يَفِرُّ الْمَرْءُ مِنْ أَخِيهِ . وَأُمِّهِ وَأَبِيهِ . وَصَاحِبَتِهِ وَبَنِيهِ}$$

"On that Day, a man shall flee from his brother, his mother, his father, his wife and his sons."

Qatādah 🕮 said, "The most beloved and then the next most beloved, and the closest of kin and then, the next closest of kin, due to the terror of that Day."

Allāh 🕮 said, **"On that Day, every one of them will be preoccupied with a predicament that will make him oblivious of another"** meaning, he will be preoccupied in his business and distracted from the affairs of others.

Ibn Abi Hātim 🕮 recorded from Sayyidunā Abdullāh Ibn Abbās 🕮 that the Holy Prophet 🕮 said, "You will all be gathered barefoot, naked and uncircumcised." So his beloved wife said, "Ya Rasoolallāh 🕮! Will we look at or see each other's nakedness?" The Holy Prophet 🕮 replied, "Every man among them on that Day will have enough (worries) to make him careless of others." Or he said, "He will be too busy to look.'"

Sayyidunā Abdullāh Ibn Abbās 🕮 narrated that the Holy Prophet 🕮 said, "You will all be gathered barefoot, naked and uncircumcised." So a woman said, "Will we see or look at each other's nakedness?" He replied, "O' so-and-so woman! Everyone among them on that Day will have enough (worries) to make him careless of others." (Tirmizi)

Referring to the faces of the pious believers, Allāh ﷻ says, **"On that Day, many faces shall be radiant, laughing and happy."** On the other hand, concerning the faces of those who forgot Allāh ﷻ in this world and continued to sin and cling to Kufr (disbelief), Allāh ﷻ says, **"And many faces will be dusty, covered in darkness."** These will be the sinful disbelievers. They will look like this because of their humiliation and fear on the Day of Judgement.

Allāh ﷻ says in Sūrah Qiyāmah,

$$وَوُجُوهٌ يَّوۡمَئِذٍ بَاسِرَةٌ ۚ تَظُنُّ أَن يُّفۡعَلَ بِهَا فَاقِرَةٌ$$

"And many faces on that Day will be gloomy, sensing that they will be dealt with most severely." (75:24-25)

Allāh ﷻ says in Sūrah Al-Imrān,

$$يَوۡمَ تَبۡيَضُّ وُجُوهٌ وَّتَسۡوَدُّ وُجُوهٌ ۚ فَأَمَّا الَّذِينَ اسۡوَدَّتۡ وُجُوهُهُمۡ أَكَفَرۡتُمۡ بَعۡدَ إِيمَانِكُمۡ$$
$$فَذُوقُوا الۡعَذَابَ بِمَا كُنۡتُمۡ تَكۡفُرُونَ ۚ وَأَمَّا الَّذِينَ ابۡيَضَّتۡ وُجُوهُهُمۡ فَفِي رَحۡمَةِ اللهِ$$
$$هُمۡ فِيهَا خَالِدُونَ$$

"The Day when some faces will be illuminated while others shall be darkened. As for those whose faces shall be darkened, it will be said to them, 'Did you disbelieve after believing? So taste the punishment because of your disbelief.' As for those whose faces shall be illuminated they will be in the mercy of Allāh, where they shall abide forever." (3:106-107)

Describing the faces of the disbelievers, Allāh ﷻ says that, they will be dusty and covered in darkness. Thus, the sin and humiliation of disbelief

96

which was hidden, will surface and become apparent on their faces. Likewise, the light and virtue of Imān which was invisible and concealed, will appear and become transparent on the faces of the believers like bright illuminated light.

Benefits Derived from this Sūrah

Before concluding the commentary of Sūrah Abas, I would like to mention some benefits and lessons we can learn from it:

1) If Prophets make any errors in their judgements, they are immediately rectified and corrected, as was the case of the Holy Prophet ﷺ with Sayyidunā Abdullāh Ibn Umm Maktoom ؓ.

2) The virtues of the pious are the shortcomings of the close ones i.e. the more close you are to Allāh ﷻ, the more precautious one has to be in terms of obedience. Even minor errors are scrutinized.

3) Not to incline towards the disbelievers even though apparently, it seems for a good purpose.

4) Not to turn away from the true, genuine believers, even though it is unintentional.

5) There is an Arabic proverb, "Until there is resentment and blame there is friendship and love. When there is no anger or reminder of shortcomings, then the friendship starts to dwindle and decline." Allāh ﷻ has the highest level of love for his beloved Prophet ﷺ, hence he reprimanded and reminded him for his shortcoming.

6) A student should not forsake seeking knowledge just because of ap-

parent barriers like in the case of Sayyidunā Abdullāh Ibn Umm Mak-toom ﷺ. Even though he was blind, poor and had no one to guide him, he made the effort to come in the presence of the Holy Prophet ﷺ to seek knowledge.

7) A teacher and guide should express love and affection for his students and impart whatever knowledge Allāh ﷻ has bestowed him with.

8) Even though the teacher or Shaykh might be of high status, if there has been any inconvenience caused by him to his juniors, disciples or stu-dents, he should not feel it below his dignity to apologise or remedy the situation. After the revelation of this Sūrah, the Holy Prophet ﷺ immedi-ately went looking for the blind Sahābi, Sayyidunā Abdullāh Ibn Umm Maktoom ﷺ, without worrying what the leaders of Makkah seated in his gathering will say. He hurried and asked for forgiveness and elevated his rank by spreading his Chādar (cloak) for him to sit down and pro-claimed: "You are my family as long as you are alive."

9) Being part of the Holy Qur'ān, this Sūrah testifies to the fact that the Holy Prophet ﷺ conveyed the complete message to the Ummah. If he feared humiliation, complaint or objection, due to being reprimanded by Allāh ﷻ, then he would not have conveyed this revelation of Sūrah Abas. In addition, Sayyidah Āishah ﷺ says, "If the Holy Prophet ﷺ wanted to conceal any revelation, then he would have concealed the incident of Sayyidah Zainab ﷺ and Sayyidunā Zaid Ibn Hāritha ﷺ, because this was a taboo subject of the time and thus another awkward incident for the Holy Prophet ﷺ which he would not have liked to be revealed. There-fore, these verses are proof of his truthfulness as a Prophet.

10) A student seeking Deeni knowledge should inculcate the quality of Taqwa as identified by Allāh ﷻ in His praises of Sayyidunā Abdullāh Ibn

Umm Maktoom ⚭ when He mentions his Taqwa. Sayyidunā Abdullāh Ibn Umm Maktoom ⚭ had the quality of Taqwa and piety in him which elevated his rank to the highest level.

May Allāh ﷻ gift us with the quality of Taqwa in our lives and beautify our lives with the Sunnāh of the Holy Prophet ﷺ. Āmeen.

Alhamdulillāh, the commentary of Sūrah Abas has been completed on the 11th of January 2014 at 1:10am, corresponding to the 9th of Rabeeul-Awwal 1435.

Bibliography

1. The Holy Qur'ān
2. Qur'ān made Easy - Mufti Afzal Hussain Ilyās
3. Ma'āriful Qur'ān - Mufti Shafi Sāhib ۞
4. Illuminating Discourses of the Noble Qur'ān - Mufti Muham-mad Āshiq Ilāhi Muhājir Madani ۞
5. Tafseer Azeezi - Shāh Abdul Aziz Muhaddith Dehlawi ۞
6. Ma'āriful Qur'ān - Maulāna Muhammad Idress Khandhlawi ۞
7. Tafseer Uthmāni - Allāmah Shabbir Ahmad Uthmāni ۞
8. The Noble Qur'ān - Dr Muhsin Khān
9. Tafseer Ibn Katheer (Abridged) - Shaykh Saifur Rahmān ۞
10. Reasons of Revelation of the Glorious Qur'ān - Abul Hasan Ali Ibn Ahmad Al-Wahidi An-Naisaburi ۞
11. Tafseer Jalālain - Imām Jalāl-Uddeen Mahalli ۞ & Imām Jalāl-Uddeen Suyooti ۞
12. Saheeh al-Bukhāri - Imām Muhammad Ibn Ismāil Al-Bukhāri ۞
13. Saheeh Muslim - Imām Muslim ۞
14. Sunan Abū Dāwood — Imām Abū Dāwood ۞
15. Sunan Nasai - Imām Nasai ۞
16. Sunan Tirmizi - Imām Tirmizi ۞
17. Sunan Ibn Mājah - Imām Ibn Mājah ۞
18. Mishkātul Masābeeh - Allāmah Baghawi ۞
19. Riyādhus Sāliheen - Imām Nawāwi ۞
20. Zādut Tālibeen - Mufti Muhammad Āshiq Ilāhi ۞
21. Pearls of Wisdom - Shayh Mufti Saiful Islām

Other titles from JKN Publications

Your Questions Answered

An outstanding book written by Shaykh Mufti Saiful Islām. A very comprehensive yet simple Fatāwa book and a source of guidance that reaches out to a wider audience i.e. the English speaking Muslims. The reader will benefit from the various answers to questions based on the Laws of Islām relating to the beliefs of Islām, knowledge, Sunnah, pillars of Islām, marriage, divorce and contemporary issues.

Hadeeth for Beginners

A concise Hadeeth book with various Ahādeeth that relate to basic Ibādāh and moral etiquettes in Islām accessible to a wider readership. Each Hadeeth has been presented with the Arabic text, its translation and commentary to enlighten the reader, its meaning and application in day-to-day life.

UK RRP: £3.00

Du'ā for Beginners

This book contains basic Du'ās which every Muslim should recite on a daily basis. Highly recommended to young children and adults studying at Islamic schools and Madrasahs so that one may cherish the beautiful treasure of supplications of our beloved Prophet ﷺ in one's daily life, which will ultimately bring peace and happiness in both worlds, Inshā-Allāh.

UK RRP: £2.00

How well do you know Islām?

An exciting educational book which contains 300 multiple questions and answers to help you increase your knowledge on Islām! Ideal for the whole family, especially children and adult students to learn new knowledge in an enjoyable way and cherish the treasures of knowledge that you will acquire from this book. A very beneficial tool for educational syllabus.

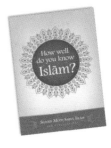

Treasures of the Holy Qur'ān

This book entitled "Treasures of the Holy Qur'ān" has been compiled to create a stronger bond between the Holy Qur'ān and the readers. It mentions the different virtues of Sūrahs and verses from the Holy Qur'ān with the hope that the readers will increase their zeal and enthusiasm to recite and inculcate the teachings of the Holy Qur'ān into their daily lives.

UK RRP: £3.00

Marriage - A Complete Solution

Islām regards marriage as a great act of worship. This book has been designed to provide the fundamental teachings and guidelines of all what relates to the marital life in a simplified English language. It encapsulates in a nutshell all the marriage laws mentioned in many of the main reference books in order to facilitate their understanding and implementation.

UK RRP: £5.00

Pearls of Luqmān

This book is a comprehensive commentary of Sūrah Luqmān, written beautifully by Shaykh Mufti Saiful Islām. It offers the reader with an enquiring mind, abundance of advice, guidance, counselling and wisdom.

The reader will be enlightened by many wonderful topics and anecdotes mentioned in this book, which will create a greater understanding of the Holy Qur'ān and its wisdom. The book highlights some of the wise sayings and words of advice Luqmān ﷺ gave to his son.

UK RRP: £3.00

Arabic Grammar for Beginners

This book is a study of Arabic Grammar based on the subject of Nahw (Syntax) in a simplified English format. If a student studies this book thoroughly, he/she will develop a very good foundation in this field, Inshā-Allāh. Many books have been written on this subject in various languages such as Arabic, Persian and Urdu. However, in this day and age there is a growing demand for this subject to be available in English .

UK RRP: £3.00

A Gift to My Youngsters

This treasure filled book, is a collection of Islamic stories, morals and anecdotes from the life of our beloved Prophet ﷺ, his Companions ﷺ and the pious predecessors. The stories and anecdotes are based on moral and ethical values, which the reader will enjoy sharing with their peers, friends, families and loved ones.

"A Gift to My Youngsters" – is a wonderful gift presented to the readers personally, by the author himself, especially with the youngsters in mind. He has carefully selected stories and anecdotes containing beautiful morals, lessons and valuable knowledge and wisdom.

UK RRP: £5.00

Travel Companion

The beauty of this book is that it enables a person on any journey, small or distant or simply at home, to utilise their spare time to read and benefit from an exciting and vast collection of important and interesting Islamic topics and lessons. Written in simple and easy to read text, this book will immensely benefit both the newly interested person in Islām and the inquiring mind of a student expanding upon their existing knowledge. Inspiring reminders from the Holy Qur'ān and the blessed words of our beloved Prophet ﷺ beautifies each topic and will illuminate the heart of the reader. **UK RRP: £5.00**

Pearls of Wisdom

Junaid Baghdādi ﷺ once said, "Allāh ﷻ strengthens through these Islamic stories the hearts of His friends, as proven from the Qur'anic verse,

"And all that We narrate unto you of the stories of the Messengers, so as to strengthen through it your heart." (11:120)

Mālik Ibn Dinār ﷺ stated that such stories are gifts from Paradise. He also emphasised to narrate these stories as much as possible as they are gems and it is possible that an individual might find a truly rare and invaluable gem among them. **UK RRP: £6.00**

Inspirations

This book contains a compilation of selected speeches delivered by Shaykh Mufti Saiful Islām on a variety of topics such as the Holy Qur'ān, Nikāh and eating Halāl. Having previously been compiled in separate booklets, it was decided that the transcripts be gathered together in one book for the benefit of the reader. In addition to this, we have included in this book, further speeches which have not yet been printed.

UK RRP: £6.00

Gift to my Sisters

A thought provoking compilation of very interesting articles including real life stories of pious predecessors, imaginative illustrations and much more. All designed to influence and motivate mothers, sisters, wives and daughters towards an ideal Islamic lifestyle. A lifestyle referred to by our Creator, Allāh ﷻ in the Holy Qur'ān as the means to salvation and ultimate success.

UK RRP: £6.00

Gift to my Brothers

A thought provoking compilation of very interesting articles including real life stories of pious predecessors, imaginative illustrations, medical advices on intoxicants and rehabilitation and much more. All designed to influence and motivate fathers, brothers, husbands and sons towards an ideal Islamic lifestyle. A lifestyle referred to by our Creator, Allāh ﷻ in the Holy Qur'ān as the means to salvation and ultimate success.

UK RRP: £5.00

Heroes of Islām

"In the narratives there is certainly a lesson for people of intelligence (understanding)." (12:111)

A fine blend of Islamic personalities who have been recognised for leaving a lasting mark in the hearts and minds of people.

A distinguishing feature of this book is that the author has selected not only some of the most world and historically famous renowned scholars but also these lesser known and a few who have simply left behind a valuable piece of advice to their nearest and dearest. **UK RRP: £5.00**

Ask a Mufti (3 volumes)

Muslims in every generation have confronted different kinds of challenges. In-spite of that, Islām produced such luminary Ulamā who confronted and re-sponded to the challenges of their time to guide the Ummah to the straight path. "Ask A Mufti" is a comprehensive three volume fatwa book, based on the Hanafi School, covering a wide range of topics related to every aspect of human life such as belief, ritual worship, life after death and contemporary legal topics related to purity, commercial transaction, marriage, divorce, food, cosmetic, laws pertaining to women, Islamic medical ethics and much more.

UK RRP: £30.00

Should I Follow a Madhab?

Taqleed or following one of the four legal schools is not a new phenomenon. Historically, scholars of great calibre and luminaries, each one being a specialist in his own right, were known to have adhered to one of the four legal schools. It is only in the previous century that a minority group emerged advocating a se-vere ban on following one of the four major schools.

This book endeavours to address the topic of Taqleed and elucidates its im-portance and necessity in this day and age. It will also, by the Divine Will of Allāh 🕮 dispel some of the confusion surrounding this topic. **UK RRP: £5.00**

Advice for the Students of Knowledge

Allāh 🕮 describes divine knowledge in the Holy Qur'ān as a 'Light'. Amongst the qualities of light are purity and guidance. The Holy Prophet 🕮 has clearly ex-plained this concept in many blessed Ahādeeth and has also taught us many supplications in which we ask for beneficial knowledge.

This book is a golden tool for every sincere student of knowledge wishing to mould his/her character and engrain those correct qualities in order to be wor-thy of receiving the great gift of Ilm from Allāh 🕮. **UK RRP: £3.00**

Stories for Children

"Stories for Children" - is a wonderful gift presented to the readers personally, by the author himself, especially with the young children in mind. The stories are based on moral and ethical values, which the reader will enjoy sharing with the peers, friends, families and loved ones. The aim is to present to the children stori and incidents which contain moral lessons, in order to reform and correct the lives, according to the Holy Qur'ān and Sunnah.

UK RRP: £5.0

Pearls from My Shaykh

This book contains a collection of pearls and inspirational accounts of the Holy Prophet ﷺ, his noble Companions, pious predecessors and some personal accounts and sayings of our well-known contemporary scholar and spiritual guide, Shaykh Mufti Saiful Islām Sāhib. Each anecdote and narrative of the pious predecessors have been written in the way that was narrated by Mufti Saiful Islām Sāhib in his discourses, drawing the specific lessons he intended from telling the story. The accounts from the life of the Shaykh has been compiled by a particular student based on their own experience and personal observation. **UK RRP: £5.00**

Paradise & Hell

This book is a collection of detailed explanation of Paradise and Hell including the state and conditions of its inhabitants. All the details have been taken from various reliable sources. The purpose of its compilation is for the reader to contemplate and appreciate the innumerable favours, rewards, comfort and unlimited luxuries of Paradise and at the same time take heed from the punishment of Hell. Shaykh Mufti Saiful Islām Sāhib has presented this book in a unique format by including the Tafseer and virtues of Sūrah Ar-Rahmān. **UK RRP: £5.00**

Prayers for Forgiveness

Prayers for Forgiveness' is a short compilation of Du'ās in Arabic, with English translation and transliteration. This book can be studied after 'Du'ā for Beginners' or as a separate book. It includes twenty more Du'ās which have not been mentioned in the previous Du'ā book. It also includes a section of Du'ās from the Holy Qur'ān and a section from the Ahādeeth. The book concludes with a section mentioning the Ninety-Nine Names of Allāh ﷻ with its translation and transliteration. **UK RRP: £3.00**

Scattered Pearls

This book is a collection of scattered pearls taken from books, magazines, emails and WhatsApp messages. These pearls will hopefully increase our knowledge, wisdom and make us realise the purpose of life. In this book, Mufti Sāhib has included messages sent to him from scholars, friends and colleagues which will be beneficial and interesting for our readers Inshā-Allāh. **UK RRP: £4.00**

Poems of Wisdom

This book is a collection of poems from those who contributed to the Al-Mumin Magazine in the poems section. The Hadeeth mentions "Indeed some form of poems are full of wisdom." The themes of each poem vary between, wittiness, thought provocation, moral lessons, emotional to name but a few. The readers will benefit from this immensely and make one ponder over the outlook of life in general.

UK RRP: £4.00